Building on Success

An Evaluation
of the
Junior Certificate
School Programme

AN ROINN DEPARTMENT OF
OIDEACHAIS EDUCATION
AGUS EOLAÍOCHTA AND SCIENCE

INSPECTORATE
Evaluation Support & Research Unit

ISBN 0-7557-7341-1

Designed by Metaphor

Photographs courtesy of Terence MacSwiney Community College, Cork.

Published by the Stationery Office

To be purchased directly from the
Government Publications Sales Office
Sun Alliance House,
Molesworth Street, Dublin 2.

   or by mail order from

Government Publications,
Postal Trade Section,
51 St. Stephen's Green, Dublin 2.
(Tel: 01-6476834   Fax: 01-6476843)

€12.00

P74704 30-01 02/06 (1,500) Brunswick Press Ltd. (15816)

Contents

Foreword by the Chief Inspector

The Junior Certificate School Programme (JCSP) is an intervention aimed at students who are potential early school leavers. It is designed to help schools to develop a student-centred approach to education and to provide students with a programme to meet their individual need. This evaluation of JCSP by the Inspectorate was designed to establish whether JCSP provided students with a positive experience of schooling, enhanced their social and personal development, improved their educational attainment and thus encouraged them to continue in full-time education. The in-school phase of the evaluation by the Inspectorate took place during the 2002/2003 school year and was designed to complement research undertaken by others in the area.

The findings of the evaluation show that the JCSP is having a positive impact in many areas. In particular, there is evidence to suggest that the programme helps to improve students' motivation and attitudes to their schooling and that it contributes to improving their literacy and numeracy skills. It is also clear that the programme has encouraged the teachers concerned to engage with a wide range of teaching methodologies and approaches and that the extra resources provided to schools for the purposes of operating the JCSP are beneficially utilised. The JCSP has also been innovative in introducing numerous initiatives into schools where teachers are facilitated with new and creative ways of working with students.

The findings also highlight a number of areas of concern that need to be addressed. These include, among others, issues concerning student selection procedures, how the JCSP curriculum is planned and reviewed and the professional development needs of the teachers involved in the delivery of the programme.

This report will contribute to consideration as to how the JCSP should be developed so that it will meet the needs of the target group. At school level all personnel involved in JCSP have a role to play in developing the JCSP in their school. The recommendations contained in this report will assist school managements and teachers in this work. At a system level the Inspectorate looks forward to engaging in discussion with schools, the relevant support services and statutory bodies about the outcomes of this evaluation. Overall, this evaluation report is intended to inform the future development of the JCSP, provide direction and guidance for schools and stimulate discussion about how best we can meet the educational needs of our students.

I would like to acknowledge the high level of co-operation the Inspectorate received from schools, teachers and the JCSP Support Service during the evaluation. I would also like to thank the Evaluation, Support and Research Unit of the Inspectorate for co-ordinating the research.

Eamon Stack

Chief Inspector

Abbreviations

ADHD	Attention-Deficit Hyperactivity Disorder
CDU	Curriculum Development Unit
CDVEC	City of Dublin Vocational Education Committee
DAS	Disadvantaged Areas Scheme
DEIS	Delivering Equality of Opportunity In Schools
ECAP	European Community Action Programme
ESS	Environmental and Social Studies
HSCL	Home-School-Community Liaison (co-ordinator)
ICD	In-Career Development
IEP	Individual Education Programme
JCSP	Junior Certificate School Programme
LCA	Leaving Certificate Applied
LCVP	Leaving Certificate Vocational Programme
NCCA	National Council for Curriculum and Assessment
NCSE	National Council for Special Education
NEPS	National Educational Psychological Service
NEWB	National Education Welfare Board
PISA	Programme for International Student Assessment
SCP	School Completion Programme
SEC	State Examinations Commission
SEN	Special Educational Needs
SESS	Special Education Support Service
SPHE	Social, Personal and Health Education
SSP	School Support Programme
SSRI	Stay-in-School Retention Initiative
STTC	Senior Traveller Training Centre
TYP	Transition Year Programme
VEC	Vocational Education Committee
WTE	Whole-time Teacher Equivalent

List of diagrams

List of tables

1 JCSP Evaluation: A Quick Look

Executive Summary

The Junior Certificate School Programme (JCSP) is an intervention within the junior cycle aimed at those students who are identified as being at risk of leaving school early, perhaps without completing the Junior Certificate. On completion of the junior cycle, JCSP students, like most other junior cycle students, receive a Junior Certificate that includes a list of the subjects taken in the Junior Certificate examination and the grades achieved in these subjects. In addition to this certificate JCSP students also receive an individualised "student profile." This is a profile of the skills, knowledge and achievements of each student. It covers a broad range of personal and social skills, in addition to academic achievements. The process of preparing this student profile lies at the core of the JCSP. Established in 1996, the JCSP now operates in 174 schools and centres for education throughout the country.

The Inspectorate of the Department of Education and Science undertook an evaluation of the JCSP in thirty schools in the school year 2002/2003. The principal objectives of the evaluation were to assess

- the JCSP curriculum in schools
- the learning and teaching methods employed in the JCSP
- the student assessment techniques employed
- the nature and quality of the planning and implementation of the programme by schools
- the extent to which schools evaluate and review their programme.

The evaluation also explored the outcomes of the JCSP in schools and the resource issues arising.

The evaluation was carried out over a period of two days in each school, during which the inspector met the principal and the JCSP co-ordinator, reviewed documents, observed lessons, interviewed key personnel in the school, and interviewed a small group of students. The inspectors also reviewed questionnaires that had been sent to the school for completion by a range of teachers before the school visit.

The following areas of the JCSP were the main focus of the evaluation:
- The organisation of the JCSP in schools
- JCSP resources
- Student selection procedures
- Student participation and retention
- The JCSP curriculum
- Teaching and learning
- Outcomes of the programme

Findings and recommendations are made regarding each of these areas. Recommendations are divided into two categories: those relating to schools and those relating to policy. The following are the main recommendations that arose from the evaluation:

Recommendations aimed at schools

- All schools should have a JCSP planning group that includes the principal, the JCSP co-ordinator, and representatives of the school's JCSP teaching team. Planning for the programme should include curriculum, assessment, resources, student selection and staffing. Each school should document its JCSP.

- Planning for students with special educational needs should take place between subject and specialist teachers.

- Schools, with the aid of the JCSP support service where necessary, should plan and implement systems, including the use of ICT, for the preparation, storage, updating and retention of JCSP records.

- Schools should keep their JCSP teaching teams as small as practicable, consistent with having enough team members with the range of skills necessary to provide an effective programme.

- Profiling should be implemented in each school's JCSP. The system should be planned, organised and co-ordinated to ensure that there is a consistent approach to it by relevant staff. Profiling should be used to inform planning for teaching and learning.

- Each school's criteria for selection of JCSP students should be documented. Records should indicate how each student is expected to benefit from the JCSP.

- Where programmes with similar objectives to those of the JCSP operate in a school, such as the School Completion Programme (SCP), the school should ensure that such programmes are co-ordinated with the JCSP so as to maximise the benefits to students.

- Schools should continue to develop and foster an awareness of the benefits of the JCSP among parents and primary schools.

- There should be follow-up by schools to the initial assessment of students. This would ensure that all students who might benefit from the JCSP can continue to participate in it, while those who might no longer require the support of the JCSP can avail of the opportunity to follow the mainstream Junior Certificate programme.

- Schools should foster regular contact between home and school. All teachers should use JCSP postcards in a systematic way.

- Schools should develop and implement a pastoral care policy or strategy for JCSP students and should provide students with guidance, including career advice, and counselling.

- School management and staff should work more closely together when developing their JCSP curriculum. The curriculum should be tailored to meet the needs and abilities of students.

- Schools should exploit the possibilities presented by ICT in both the administration of the programme and in learning and teaching.

- Irish Cultural Studies courses should supplement, and not replace, the study of Irish in the JCSP. Where relevant, schools should review the place of Irish Cultural Studies in their JCSP curriculum and give consideration to including foundation level Junior Certificate Irish.

- The practice by some schools of shortening the school day for JCSP students should be discontinued.

- Each school providing the JCSP should develop whole-school literacy and numeracy strategies. Greater attention needs to be given to the development of these skills in the classroom.

- The development of students' social and personal skills should continue to be an emphasis of the JCSP.

- Evidence of students' progress, including the achievement of learning targets, should be accessible to students, teachers, and parents alike.

- Greater attention needs to be given to monitoring students' attendance and punctuality in lessons. Schools should devise a system of centrally administering attendance and punctuality data and communicating it with the home.
- All teaching and learning in the JCSP should have clarity of purpose, provide opportunities for students' participation and take account of student assessment outcomes.
- The outcomes of assessment should inform the selection of profiling statements and learning targets. Students should be made aware of their progress in all subject areas.
- Schools should devise ways of continuously recognising students' effort and achievement.

Recommendations aimed at policy advisers and policy-makers

- The JCSP student profiling system should be subjected to a thorough review with a view to exploring ways of reducing the administrative requirement of the programme on schools.
- Given the significant workload involved in co-ordinating the JCSP, particularly in those schools where large numbers of JCSP students are enrolled, consideration should be given to revising the additional whole-time teacher equivalent allocation currently made available to schools.
- Consideration needs to be given to providing special schools with some additional allocation of teaching time.
- The funding arrangements currently in place for the JCSP should be reviewed and should be considered in light of funding made available for other initiatives and programmes in schools.
- The JCSP Support Service should undertake a review of the strategies employed in the delivery of In-Career Development provision associated with the programme. There is also a need for more in-career development courses in the area of special educational needs.
- The JCSP Support Service, in conjunction with the National Educational Psychological Service, should develop and disseminate appropriate guidelines to schools on best practice for the selection of students for the JCSP, including the assessment instruments to be used.
- Consideration should be given to how JCSP can best continue to meet the needs of post-primary students with special education needs. The Special Education Support Service (SESS) and the JCSP Support Service, in collaboration with other relevant stakeholders, should address this issue.
- Guidelines on the provision of guidance and counselling within the JCSP should be developed for schools.
- School records of students' attendance and their destination after completing the junior cycle should be aggregated nationally in order to determine the success of the JCSP at improving attendance and retention.
- The National Council for Curriculum and Assessment, in collaboration with the JCSP Support Service, should develop and support the implementation of suitable programmes in modern European languages for the JCSP.
- The JCSP Support Service should investigate how the use of ICT in the JCSP could be substantially developed in order to support teaching and learning.
- Teaching methodologies need to be tailored more to the needs and interests of students. Teachers should be supported in this task by a whole-school emphasis on quality in teaching and learning. The JCSP Support Service can play an important role in this area.

2   JCSP – The Story
The Junior Certificate School Programme

2.1   Introduction

Typically, students are about twelve years of age on entry to second-level education, and they sit a Junior Certificate examination at the end of a three-year junior cycle. The Junior Certificate School Programme (JCSP) is a Department of Education and Science intervention within the junior cycle. While the majority of institutions providing the JCSP are post-primary schools, it is also provided in a range of education centres, including Senior Traveller Training Centres (STTCs), special schools, remand centres and Youth Encounter projects.

The JCSP is predominantly aimed at those students who are identified as being at risk of leaving school early, perhaps without completing the Junior Certificate. By identifying the factors that lead to students leaving school early, and incorporating principles and practices designed to address these problems, the JCSP seeks to retain students in school and to give them an experience of success while at school. It is based on the principle that, when properly supported, all young people are capable of achievement and success.

On completion of the junior cycle, JCSP students, like other junior cycle students, receive a Junior Certificate that includes a list of the subjects taken in the state examination and the grades achieved in those subjects. JCSP students, however, also receive an individualised *Student Profile* which outlines the skills, knowledge and achievements that they have attained during the course of the programme. The profile covers a broad range of personal and social skills, in addition to academic achievements. The process of preparing this profile lies at the core of the JCSP.

As part of the student profiling system, students achieve short-term goals in academic, social and personal development. This process gives them a frequent experience of success, thus enhancing their experience of school and providing an incentive for continued efforts. The JCSP provides a curriculum framework and a method of working with students that enables schools and teachers to adopt a student-centred approach to help students benefit from their time at school.

2.2   Origin and Development of the JCSP

The JCSP has its origins in the Early School Leavers' Project initiated by the City of Dublin VEC through its Curriculum Development Unit (CDU). This project was established in 1979 as part of the European Community Action Programme entitled "Transition from Education to Working Life." The terms of reference of the project were:

- to identify early school leavers, namely those students who derive little or no benefit from their schooling, who leave school at the earliest opportunity, and who are unprepared for the world of work and consequently either drift from one job to another or remain more or less permanently unemployed
- to design, implement and evaluate a curriculum suitable to the needs of these students

The following activities and methods were included in the project:

- research
- in-service training
- student profiling
- links between primary and post-primary school
- assessment and certification procedures
- links with employers
- links with parents
- work exploration
- the development of student materials

The project sought to provide a course for students that would be stimulating and directly related to their needs. It also sought to prepare students for the world of work and adult responsibility and to provide them with a positive record of achievement at school.

Following a pilot phase, in September 1996 the Department of Education and Science launched the Junior Certificate School Programme in thirty-two schools. It was originally called the Junior Certificate Elementary Programme. Development work on this new programme was carried out by the CDU of the City of Dublin VEC, in consultation with the National Council for Curriculum and Assessment (NCCA) and the Department of Education and Science. From the original thirty-two schools in the pilot phase the number of schools and other centres of education offering the JCSP had grown to 174 in 2005.

This figure breaks down as follows:

- 139 post-primary schools
- 15 special schools
- 8 Senior Traveller Training Centres
- 5 Youth Encounter Projects
- 4 Remand centres
- 3 schools catering for students with physical disabilities/deafness

Up to 2003 only those post-primary schools that participated in the Department of Education and Science Disadvantaged Areas Scheme (DAS)[1] were permitted to offer the JCSP. In the 2002/2003 school year there were 203 post-primary schools participating in the DAS. Since then, however, those schools that participate in the School Completion Programme (SCP) are permitted to offer the JCSP. Figures for the 2004/2005 school year show that 112 post-primary schools participate in the SCP. This programme is a project of the Department of Education and Science that aims to have a significant positive impact on levels of student retention in primary and post-primary schools and on the numbers of students who successfully complete their senior cycle. The programme started out as two separate programmes: (i) the 8 to 15 Early School Leaver Initiative, and (ii) the Stay-in-School Retention Initiative (SSRI). The SCP is a central component of the Department's strategy of discriminating positively in favour of children and young people who are at risk of, or who are experiencing, educational disadvantage. The programme is funded on a multi-annual basis under the National Development Plan, with assistance from the European Social Fund.

---

1 The Disadvantaged Areas Scheme of the Department of Education and Science benefits some 203 schools serving approx 96,000 pupils by providing over quota teaching posts, additional funding to launch book rental schemes, additional student capitation grants and a home/school liaison grant to develop links with parents. In the case of VEC schools and colleges, additional capitation funding corresponding to that for other schools, is built into the regular funding arrangements for VECs.

In June 2005 the Minister for Education and Science launched a new action plan for education inclusion. DEIS, or Delivering Equality Of Opportunity In Schools, (Department of Education and Science, 2005) proposes a new integrated School Support Programme (SSP) which will bring together and build upon existing interventions for schools and school clusters/communities with a concentrated level of educational disadvantage. The SCP is one of a number of existing schemes and programmes that will be integrated into the SSP over the five-year implementation period of DEIS. At second-level, schools identified for participation in the SSP will benefit from additional supports including:

● Access to the Junior Certificate School Programme and the Leaving Certificate Applied and associated staffing and funding supports
● Additional non-pay/capitation allocation based on the level of disadvantage
● Increased funding under the School Book Grant Scheme for establishing, developing and ongoing support of book loan/rental schemes
● Access to Home School Community Liaison Scheme services
● Access to a range of supports (both academic and non-academic) to retain young people in school
● Access to transfer programmes supporting progression from primary to second-level education
● Access to planning supports
● Access to a range of professional development supports

These measures will be extended to second-level schools in the School Support Programme on a phased basis.

Fig. 2.1, which illustrates student participation, shows the growth of JCSP from forty eight students in the pilot phase in 1996 to 5466 students in 2004. The number of students enrolled in each of the academic years highlighted refers to all students in the first, second and third year of the programme in that academic year.

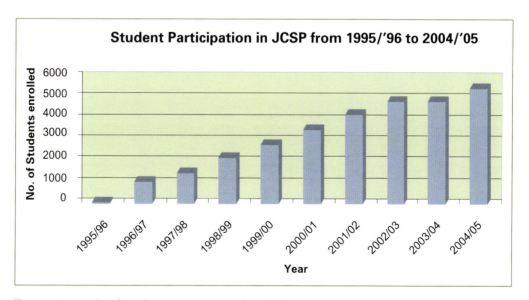

Figure 2.1   Student Participation in the JCSP, 1996–2004

In June 2004, of the 56,865 candidates that sat for the Junior Certificate examination, 1,627 were participants in the JCSP. Table 2.1 lists the 21 subjects in which JCSP students sat the Junior Certificate examination that year and the number of students for each subject.

Subject	Number of candidates
English	1588
Mathematics	1573
Civic, Social & Personal Education (CSPE)	1397
Art, Craft & Design	1140
Irish	1008
Home Economics	850
Material Technology (Wood)	782
Science	635
Metalwork	629
Environmental and Social Studies (ESS)	401
Business Studies	306
Technical Graphics	301
French	144
Music	127
Religious Education	115
Science (with local studies)	101
Italian	77
Technology	61
Spanish	27
German	16
Typewriting	16

Table 2.1   Subjects taken by JCSP students in the Junior Certificate examination (2004)

2.3   JCSP Target Group

It has been estimated that about one thousand young people do not transfer from primary school to post-primary school each year (National Economic and Social Forum (NESF), 1997). Also, significant numbers of students fail to progress through the education system. According to the NESF (2002), for example, of those students who entered second-level education in September 1994, 2,400 left with no formal qualification. Of those who sat their Junior Certificate examination in 1997, 10,600 did not sit the Leaving Certificate in 1999 or 2000. In all, at the end of the 1990's about 13,000 young people – approximately one-fifth of the total student cohort at that time – were leaving school annually without having sat for the Leaving Certificate examination.

Further, according to the NESF (2002) report, a high proportion of young people who leave full-time education before completing the junior cycle come from families of semi-skilled or unskilled backgrounds. These students, it states, are more likely to become unemployed than those leaving school with a qualification and they are also less likely to return to education. According to the Conference of Religious in Ireland (1997), "an adult with no educational qualification is nine times more likely to be poor than someone with third level education" (p.21).

A number of factors have been identified as predictors of early school leaving. According to the NESF (2002) these can include under-achievement and low academic performance, poor self-esteem and experiences of bullying, unsuitable school curricular programmes and disciplinary procedures, drug or alcohol use, problems in students' homes, the attraction of easily obtained employment, absenteeism from school, poor student-teacher relations, school transport issues and a lack of engagement between school and students.

The JCSP is aimed at those students who are affected by these kinds of factors. The target group for the JCSP are students who:

- have repeatedly experienced failure during their schooling and suffer from lack of confidence or low self-esteem
- have serious difficulties with basic skills, including literacy and numeracy, that interfere with their ability to cope with the normal demands of school and of everyday life
- may be at risk of leaving school before the end of the junior cycle

Schools generally set down criteria for the selection of students for the JCSP. Good practice entails giving priority to the students' most likely to leave school early. While the majority of schools select students for the JCSP on entry, in other schools they are selected during first year, following a period of assessment in the school.

2.4   Aims of the JCSP

The JCSP seeks to retain students in school through addressing factors that are linked to early school leaving. As already mentioned, this is based on the premise that if students can be given an experience of success while at school they are more likely to remain in school, at least until they have completed their Junior Certificate examination.

The JCSP is designed to enhance students' social and personal development, support them in achieving in the Junior Certificate programme, remedy deficits in their academic development and encourage them to identify with and gain satisfaction from being in school. It aims to do this through having a small group of school staff interacting daily with students, with the needs of each student being at the centre of the planning and teaching of the programme. There is an emphasis on identifying these needs and evaluating the extent to which they are being met by the programme through regular assessment and feedback to students.

By addressing systematically the identified correlates of early school leaving, the JCSP aims to prolong the length of time students spend in the education system, thus improving their life and career prospects. Ultimately, through improvement in the general educational level of the work force, the JCSP contributes towards helping with the economic development of the country.

2.5 Best Practice in Schools/Centres for Education

Best practice in relation to the operation of the JCSP in schools/centres for education calls for effective management of the programme, effective delivery of the programme in the classroom and effective student assessment and student profiling structures and procedures.

Management of the JCSP

The JCSP in a post-primary school will generally have a co-ordinator who is responsible for the implementation of the programme and has a specific time allocation (which varies between schools depending on the level of student participation) for carrying out this work. An effective programme will have an annual cycle which includes planning of the programme and assessment of students' achievements. As part of their work co-ordinators regularly meet with staff members, students and parents. Early in the school year the whole-school thrust of the JCSP is usually emphasised through a presentation to the staff of the programme for the year. Teachers who are new to the JCSP are inducted into the programme and the initial planning for that year's programme takes place. There can also be an information meeting for parents, though frequently parents will have been briefed while their children were in primary school. As the year progresses the JCSP co-ordinator is also involved in documenting and keeping records relating to the programme.

The co-ordinator generally belongs to a JCSP planning team and this team may include, among others, some subject teachers, resource and learning-support teachers, the school guidance counsellor, the HSCL teacher and the School Completion Programme (SCP) co-ordinator. The JCSP planning team may involve itself in student selection, curricular and resource planning issues and could be said to have day-to-day responsibility for the running of the programme. Because of the need for a team approach in meeting the needs of students there is usually close collaboration between JCSP subject teachers and specialist teachers, such as resource and learning-support teachers, and the school's guidance counsellor. The school's JCSP co-ordinator is best placed to facilitate this collaboration through effective communication and team working.

During the school year there are usually a number of celebrations, for example at Christmas and at the presentation of profiles at the end of third year. Parents and members of the school staff not directly involved in the programme are frequently invited to these, thereby raising the profile of the programme in the school. Students also frequently take part in competitions, many of which are organised by the JCSP Support Service.

JCSP in the Classroom

The emphasis in a JCSP classroom is placed on the personal and social development of students with student involvement in group and outdoor activities, and regular student affirmation. In order to make this more effective, small class sizes are provided where possible.

Teachers engage their students in active learning and use a variety of teaching methods. Students often take a number of subjects that are practically based. Many take a reduced number of examination subjects in their Junior Certificate, and this helps to create time for social and personal development activities and for the other activities associated with the programme. Students receive individual attention, good behaviour is affirmed and inappropriate behaviour is dealt with in a fair and consistent manner.

A strong emphasis is placed on meeting the learning needs of students, in particular the improvement of literacy and numeracy skills. To this end there is a high degree of involvement by learning-support teachers and, where available, resource teachers. Appropriate reading materials are made available to support the development of literacy.

The JCSP strives to improve students' attendance and punctuality through forming strong links with students' homes. The school's home-school-community liaison (HSCL) co-ordinator, where available, has a key role to play in enhancing the relationship between school and home. Effective home-school linkage entails schools keeping parents or guardians continually informed of students' progress, JCSP activities being given a high profile in the school, and parents being invited to attend JCSP events. These events usually celebrate work that students have carried out during the year.

Student Assessment and Profiling Structures

The JCSP has at its core a system of student profiling that provides students with a record of their achievements. Before an initial planning meeting, which is generally held some six to eight weeks into the first term in the school year, each JCSP teacher, or the members of the JCSP teaching team, select 'profiling statements', commonly referred to as 'statements', to be achieved or completed by students. A profiling statement is a general description of a particular area of knowledge, ability or skill. Essentially, a statement affirms that a student knows, understands or can do something and teachers, by the time of the initial planning meeting, will be aware of the strengths and needs of their students. Statements can be either subject specific (sometimes referred to as subject-based) or cross-curricular in nature. The subject-specific statements reflect many of the aims and objectives of the Junior Certificate subject syllabi. Cross-curricular statements on the other hand are not subject-specific but are aimed at enhancing the JCSP students' social and personal skills (such as punctuality and co-operation), as well as non-subject specific academic competencies. At the planning meeting agreement is generally reached on the statements to be completed by individual students.

Each statement is defined or described by a series of 'learning targets'. Learning targets are specific, short-term goals that lead to a statement. They outline the steps that are followed and the material that should be covered if the student is to achieve competence in the long-term target, the statement. The selection of targets is based on the individual student's needs and abilities and best practise entails the teacher involving the student in the selection of the particular learning targets to be attempted or completed for any particular statement. To achieve a statement all targets must be completed and students are regularly assessed on the achievement or otherwise of these learning targets. Students receive feedback and acknowledgement of success.

An example of a subject specific statement and two associated learning targets is given in Fig. 2.2, while an example of a cross-curricular statement and two associated learning targets is given in Fig. 2.3.

Home Economics **Food and Culinary skills** At Junior Certificate level the student can: **Plan, prepare, cook and present simple, well-balanced meals for individuals and groups** **Learning Targets** This has been demonstrated by your ability to: 1. Follow a simple recipe 2. Weigh and measure food using the correct equipment etc. ■ ❑ ❑ Work began ■ ■ ❑ Work in progress ■ ■ ■ Work completed	**Social Competence** **Speaking** At Junior Certificate level the student can: **Use the spoken word to accurately express opinions and experiences in a social context** **Learning Targets** This has been demonstrated by your ability to: 1. Leave a message on a telephone answering machine 2. Relay instructions and messages accurately etc. ■ ❑ ❑ Work began ■ ■ ❑ Work in progress ■ ■ ■ Work completed

Fig. 2.2 Subject specific profiling statement and two associated learning targets

Fig. 2.3 Cross-curricular profiling statement and two associated learning targets

Profiling statements are available for each subject, and through them the Junior Certificate syllabus is broken into small units. These statements and targets are generally awarded by subject teachers. Cross-curricular statements and learning targets may be awarded either by individual teachers or following discussion between groups of teachers.

During the school year a number of profiling meetings are held (usually around December, February and April). A profile meeting is a meeting of the JCSP teachers and such meetings are usually organised by the JCSP co-ordinator. The purpose of these meetings is to update the records for a particular group of students. Teachers discuss the progress of each student and recommend which students have completed enough work to be awarded statements. At the end of third year, and before the Junior Certificate examination, students receive their JCSP profile. A student profile is a positive record of statements that a student is working on or has achieved and will have been compiled throughout the junior cycle.

2.6   Department of Education and Science Support

Schools approved for participation in the JCSP are restricted to a maximum of 45 approved places in each of the three years of the junior cycle. Participating schools receive an improved teaching allocation from the Department of Education and Science. At present the allocation is at the rate of 0.25 whole-time teacher equivalent (WTE) (or 5.5. hours per week) per group of forty-five students participating in the JCSP. So, schools with forty-five JCSP pupils or fewer receive an allocation of 0.25 WTE, schools with forty-six to ninety students receive an allocation of 0.50 WTE, while schools with ninety-one to 135 JCSP students receive an allocation of 0.75 WTE. This time allocation is provided for co-ordination activities and for meetings associated with the programme. Schools also receive a once-off grant in respect of each student enrolled on the programme. (See Appendix 1 for details of supports.)

A specialist JCSP Support Service is based in the CDU of the City of Dublin VEC. The support service develops JCSP support materials and also provides advice and professional development for teachers. It organises training events for JCSP co-ordinators as well as a wide range of other meetings and courses for subject teachers. Along with introductory sessions for individual schools, the JCSP Support Service has also over the past few years provided support to schools on literacy, JCSP self-evaluation by schools, mathematics, and on identifying and accommodating the learning styles of students.

The JCSP Support Service, in collaboration with schools, certifies the profiling of students. Essentially, this entails the school, usually the JCSP co-ordinator, sending information to the JCSP Support Service which indicates the full list of statements to be awarded to individual students. The support service prepares a presentation folder for each student which includes a certificate of participation validated by the Department of Education and Science and a list of statements completed by that particular student. The presentation folders are returned to the schools. Students are usually presented with their final profiles at a graduation or award ceremony, as referred to in section 2.5. As can be seen, the support service has a central role in the administration, support and development of the JCSP.

3 Under the Lens

Evaluation of the Junior Certificate School Programme

3.1 Introduction

This chapter describes the background to the evaluation of the JCSP carried out by the Inspectorate. The purpose and aims of the evaluation are explained and the methodology used for the evaluation is described. An outline of the reporting procedures that pertained to the evaluation in schools is also given.

3.2 Context for the evaluation of the JCSP by the Inspectorate

In 1989 a new curriculum was introduced for students in the Junior cycle of post-primary schools. Ten years later, in 1999, the NCCA published its review of that new curriculum – *Progress Report: Issues and Options for Development* (1999). Here, the junior cycle was reviewed in terms of its aims and objectives, the manner in which it was structured and assessed and the extent to which it had been successful in meeting the needs of all students. One of the recommendations made by the NCCA in their 1999 report was that they themselves should undertake a review of the JCSP "with a view to it being given greater support at school and national level and being made more widely available" (p.28). The NCCA report also recommended that there should be greater availability of the programme for those students who have difficulty with mainstream junior cycle education.

Before the start of an evaluation of the JCSP by the Inspectorate, and as part of the NCCAs own review of the JCSP, the Department of Education and Science and the NCCA commissioned independent research on the JCSP[2]. This research was in support of the objectives of the NCCAs review of the JCSP, which were to:

- assess the effectiveness of the JCSP for potential early school leavers
- provide the NCCA with data on the effectiveness of the structure, format and content of the JCSP

This research involved consultation with stakeholders to evaluate the development and impact of the programme. The principals of all JCSP schools and centres for education providing the programme were surveyed, and study visits were made to a range of schools and centres. Data were also gathered on JCSP students in those schools and in particular on the subjects taken by them in the Junior Certificate examination.

---

2 Nexus, (2002), *Research in Support of the Review of the Junior Certificate School Programme*, (unpublished report).

3.3 Purpose and aims of the evaluation

After the review of the JCSP by the NCCA, which involved the joint commissioning of independent research by the NCCA and the Department of Education and Science, the Inspectorate carried out its own evaluation of the JCSP. The evaluation of the JCSP by the Inspectorate took place during the 2002/2003 school year and aimed to complement the work of the independently commissioned research, and to gain further comprehensive and reliable information on the implementation and effectiveness of the programme.

The principal objectives of the evaluation of the JCSP carried out by the Inspectorate were to evaluate the:

- JCSP curriculum in schools
- teaching and learning methods employed in the JCSP
- assessment techniques employed
- nature and quality of the planning and implementation of the programme by schools
- extent to which schools evaluate and review their programme
- outcomes of the JCSP in schools and resource issues arising.

3.4 Overview of the evaluation procedure

All 138 schools and centres for education providing the JCSP in the 2001/2002 school year were notified in May 2002 of the Inspectorates' forthcoming evaluation of the programme. A total of thirty schools were subsequently selected for participation. The schools were selected randomly to be representative of all school types offering the programme. Two of the thirty schools selected for participation were special schools. The schools were informed of their selection during the period September/October 2002. The in-school phase of the evaluation was undertaken during the period October–December 2002.

The evaluation team comprised sixteen inspectors and shortly before the evaluation visits in the October–December 2002 period all thirty schools were visited to brief the principal on the evaluation process. In some instances the JCSP co-ordinator was also briefed. These pre-evaluation visits allowed for timetabling arrangements for the evaluation visit to be made. Also, a series of questionnaires aimed at various school personnel involved in the JCSP were left with the principal and co-ordinator at this time. These were to be completed by the relevant personnel and would be collected by the inspector during the evaluation visit.

The evaluation itself was carried out over a period of two days in each school, during which one/two inspector(s) interviewed the Principal, the JCSP co-ordinator and other relevant school personnel, including a small group of JCSP students. Inspectors also observed lessons and reviewed relevant school documents, including the questionnaires that had been provided for completion by school personnel prior to the evaluation visit. The thirty school evaluation visits yielded the data sources indicated in Table 3.1.

Data source	Number of each
Responses to subject teacher questionnaire	169
Class observation form	135
School report	30
Evaluation instrument	30
Responses to co-ordinator questionnaire	30
Responses to resource teacher questionnaire	25
Responses to home-school-community liaison teacher questionnaire	22
Responses to learning-support teacher questionnaire	22
Responses to guidance counsellor questionnaire	19
Responses to SCP co-ordinator questionnaire	19
Interviews with students	16
Review of school records	16
Interview with Principal	14
Interview with specialist teachers	14

Table 3.1   Data sources for national evaluation of the JCSP

In January 2003 the inspectors revisited each school to convey the outcome of the evaluation to the principal and JCSP co-ordinator, giving them the opportunity to clarify facts and to respond to the evaluation findings. Individual reports were issued to schools in May 2003.

A follow-up to the evaluation took place in April 2004, and twenty-nine of the thirty schools/centres for education involved in the evaluation participated. Before the follow-up, schools were requested to submit a report to the Department of Education and Science on the progress they had made at implementing the recommendations in their JCSP evaluation report. They were asked to rate themselves, on a scale of 1 to 4, on progress made regarding their specific recommendations. (Details of the outcome of this follow-up evaluation are provided in Appendix 2.)

3.4.1   Questionnaires

As part of the evaluation, questionnaires were completed by JCSP co-ordinators, guidance counsellors, resource teachers, learning-support teachers, subject teachers, SCP co-ordinators and, where available, HSCL teachers. The purpose of the questionnaires was to ascertain different viewpoints and quantitative data on the functioning of the JCSP in schools. Analysis of the data provided an overview of the responses of the different categories of teachers. Among the issues dealt with in the questionnaires were:

- the planning and organising of the programme
- students with special educational needs
- curriculum
- cross-curricular activities
- student profiling

- resources
- in-career development
- home-school links

3.4.2 Interviews

During the in-school phase of the evaluation, inspectors conducted interviews with school personnel, including the school principal, a group of specialist staff involved in the JCSP (learning-support teachers, resource teachers, SCP co-ordinators, guidance counsellors and HSCL-teachers) and a group of five or six students following the JCSP (generally third-year students). Each interview lasted approximately forty minutes.

3.4.3 School records

The inspectors reviewed relevant documentary records held in schools. These included planning documents, timetables for classes, curriculum documents, records of team meetings, student profiling records, records of JCSP activities and communications with parents. This part of the evaluation provided useful information on the range and availability of school records in relation to the JCSP.

3.4.4 Observation of teaching and learning

Between five and seven lessons were observed in each of the thirty schools. Inspectors used a set of common indicators to evaluate the quality of the lessons. These included:

- planning of lessons and resources
- teaching methods and materials
- literacy and numeracy
- social and personal statements
- catering for individual students' needs
- monitoring of attendance
- quality of learning taking place

Data from each of the lessons observed were recorded and analysed to provide an overall picture at national level.

3.5 Reporting to Schools

As referred to earlier, each school that participated in the evaluation received an evaluation report. These reports referred to the following aspects of the JCSP:

- planning and review
- student selection process
- organisation and management
- maximising students' participation and retention
- curriculum
- learning and teaching
- assessment
- outcomes of the JCSP in the school.

A summary of the main findings and recommendations for further development of each school's JCSP was included in the reports.

4   Making the JCSP Work

Organisation of the JCSP in Schools

4.1   Introduction

This chapter examines the organisational issues involved in the provision of the JCSP in those schools that participated in the evaluation. It examines teamwork in the JCSP, and in so doing gives particular focus to the areas of programme planning, programme organisation and implementation and the quality of teaching in the programme. The role of the co-ordinator is also examined, as well as the extent to which review of the programme takes place in schools. Finally, the chapter looks at how JCSP classes are formed and organised, as well as issues regarding timetabling and subject choice for students.

4.2   Teamwork in the JCSP

A number of specific tasks or areas of work can be identified with regard to the operation of the JCSP in a school. These include:

- planning
- organising and implementing
- teaching

It was found that some schools had separate teams for engaging with each of these tasks, while others had fewer teams. The following three teams were identified in schools:

1. the *planning team*: this team can be involved in planning for the introduction of the JCSP into a school, along with other planning activities throughout the year
2. the *JCSP team*: this team meets regularly and carries out the profiling of students
3. the *teaching team*: this is the group of JCSP teachers in a school.

The composition of these three teams overlapped and varied between schools. In some schools, for example, the *JCSP team* and the *teaching team* had the same membership, while in others the *planning team* and the *JCSP team* were the same. In a number of schools it was found that all three teams were the same.

4.2.1   The Planning Team

Planning can take place at different levels within the JCSP. In those schools evaluated planning was observed at three distinct levels:

- planning that takes place when the JCSP is being introduced by a school into its curriculum
- planning that takes place before the start of each school year
- planning that takes place during each school year.

When planning for the introduction of the JCSP into a school, good practice involves decisions being made by a planning team on the manner in which students are to be selected for the programme, and on the curriculum that is to be offered to them. In the case of the curriculum, as well as addressing issues such as the subjects to be included and the teachers to be involved, schools also plan for resources for the programme. It is considered that the quality of this initial planning had a substantial influence on the quality of the programme in a school.

It was found that the school principal or deputy principal, or both, collaborated with the JCSP co-ordinator, and the planning team, to plan the programme in thirty-seven per cent of those schools that participated in the evaluation. Eighty-one per cent of these schools involved teachers in planning for the programme and in the majority of these it included an involvement by the guidance counsellor, the learning-support teacher, the HSCL co-ordinator, the resource teacher and the SCP co-ordinator (where available in the school). Fig. 4.1 gives an indication of the personnel involved in planning the JCSP in schools.

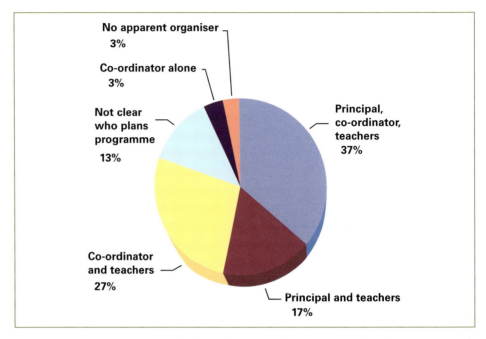

Figure 4.1 Personnel involved in planning the JCSP in schools

Given the importance of planning at this stage, it is considered essential that the school principal be a member of any group planning for the introduction of the JCSP. Also, to ensure continuity from planning to implementation, the JCSP co-ordinator should also be a member of this group.

The JCSP also requires careful and continual planning throughout the school year. This planning can include the induction of new teachers into the programme, informing parents about the programme, individual planning by teachers, deciding on profiling statements for students, planning JCSP events, monitoring students' progress, compiling student profiles at the end of the school year and planning initiatives and projects such as Make-a-Book[3] and Readalong[4]. It was found that practically all JCSP schools held a planning meeting at the start of each school year, and that most held other JCSP team meetings on average about once a term. While these latter team meetings were mainly concerned with the running of the programme and managing the profiling system, they also incorporated a planning function. Further consideration of the team involved in this kind of work is included in Section 4.2.2.

3 'Make-a-Book' is a project organised by the JCSP Support Service with the assistance of the staff of the Curriculum Development Unit. It aims to develop cross-curricular work in schools by asking students, in groups, to develop their own storybooks. A national awards event is held each year to celebrate students' achievements in the project.

4 'Readalong' is an initiative aimed at students with a reading age below 9–10 years. It involves the use of personal tape recorders and audio books in school to support students' reading. The initiative offers schools a grant to buy a Readalong kit – a set of personal tape recorders and a selection of books and accompanying tapes – for a group of JCSP students. Co-ordinators are given an information pack outlining the use of Readalong and listing the suppliers of suitable materials.

Table 4.1 lists the principal planning activities undertaken by 169 JCSP subject teachers who responded to an evaluation questionnaire.

Planning activity	Proportion of teachers
Deciding on students' profiling statements	81.1%
Planning in own subject area only	77.9%
Planning for a particular class or year group	61.5%
Planning and formulating the school's JCSP plan	43.4%
Selecting students for participation in the JCSP	23.7%
Planning (other), e.g. cross-curricular activities and JCSP meetings and outings	21.9%

Table 4.1   JCSP planning activities engaged in by subject teachers

It is evident from this table that most of the planning activities of subject teachers involved in the JCSP are in relation to their own class groups.

Thirty per cent of the subject teachers expressed a desire for greater involvement in JCSP planning, particularly with regard to more time for meetings to develop cross-curricular statements and to review students' progress. When asked about the quality of their schools' planning for the JCSP, teachers stated that more time for meetings to plan and carry out profiling was needed. Almost all resource teachers stated in their questionnaire responses that they were involved in planning for students with special educational needs.

In their reports, inspectors made recommendations relating to planning for the JCSP in up to half of the schools evaluated. The most frequent recommendation was that planning should be informed by the outcomes of regular internal reviews of the JCSP. It was also frequently recommended that planning should adopt a whole school approach, or that it should at least involve all the key JCSP personnel in a school. Further, it was frequently recommended that the planning process associated with the programme be documented. In particular, inspectors' suggested that written plans should be adopted by all of those schools providing the JCSP. Finally, it was sometimes found that schools providing the JCSP could make more effective use of their additional teaching time allocation by allocating teachers some planning time for the programme. It was suggested, for example, that a planning group, which should include the principal, JCSP co-ordinator and other members of the school's JCSP teaching team, should be established.

4.2.2   The JCSP Team

From the inspectors' observations it is evident that there was considerable variation in the composition of the JCSP team in schools. This was usually the group responsible for the effective running of the JCSP, including the profiling of students. As shown in Table 4.2, of the thirty schools evaluated, only twenty-two, or seventy-three per cent, had an identifiable and functioning JCSP team. Unless schools had properly constituted teams that met regularly, it was difficult to see how the important activities of the JCSP could be carried out effectively. However, as reported by school principals during the evaluation, it was also recognised that many do experience difficulty in balancing meeting time with teaching time.

It was common practice for JCSP team meetings to take place during the school day. In such cases teachers were sometimes released from lessons to attend. A number of schools reported dealing with JCSP planning matters at regular staff meetings throughout the year, while a small number of schools held JCSP meetings outside class time (e.g., at lunch time). Six of those schools evaluated were found to hold no regular meetings during the year and further, it was found that a small number of schools close, or send students home, to allow for formal meetings of JCSP personnel. Closing a school to facilitate JCSP profiling meetings is poor practice, and one that is not in the interest of students.

The JCSP Team	Number of schools
Size from six to twenty, including most JCSP teachers	13
No team; appear to be run by one person, generally either the principal or JCSP co-ordinator	8
Co-ordinator and one or two others, usually the principal or deputy principal and sometimes the guidance counsellor	5
Co-ordinator and some combination of learning-support teacher, guidance counsellor, HSCL teacher, SCP co-ordinator	4

Table 4.2   Composition of school's JCSP team by number of schools

Along with meetings of the entire JCSP team in a school, there were also meetings of smaller groups of JCSP teachers to plan various activities within the JCSP. Table 4.3 details the frequency of meetings of the JCSP team, or smaller groups of teachers, in the thirty schools visited by inspectors.

Group	Weekly	Monthly	Once a term	Once or twice a year	Never
Entire JCSP team	8.3%	4.2%	58.3%	20.8%	8.3%
Smaller groups of teachers	44.0%	28.0%	8.0%	8.0%	12.0%

Table 4.3   Frequency of meetings of JCSP school personnel

The frequency of meetings varied widely, with fifty-eight per cent of teams meeting once a term, and only twelve-and-a-half per cent meeting more often. In a number of schools meetings took place only once or twice a year, or never. Smaller groups of teachers tended to meet more frequently in an informal manner. In eight schools visited as part of the evaluation inspectors recommended that team meetings be scheduled, or that sufficient time be allocated for such meetings.

Schools should allow time for holding at least one meeting of the JCSP team per term to plan for and run the JCSP. Other meetings should be held to induct teachers new to the JCSP, to inform staff members about the JCSP, and to enhance contact with the parents of JCSP students.

Table 4.4 provides some insights into what happens in JCSP team meetings. It is noteworthy that while nearly two-thirds of co-ordinators considered that the number of meetings held was usually adequate, fewer than half considered that there was usually enough time at meetings to discuss the progress of individual students. In nearly two-thirds of schools visited, all JCSP teachers generally attended profiling meetings.

Issue	Always	Usually	Sometimes	Never
The number of JCSP profiling meetings held each year is adequate	29.6%	33.3%	22.2%	14.8%
Sufficient time is available at JCSP profiling meetings to discuss each student's progress	21.4%	25.0%	28.6%	25.0%
JCSP team meetings select statements for students	29.6%	25.9%	33.3%	11.1%
All JCSP teachers attend profiling meetings	17.9%	46.4%	21.4%	14.3%
JCSP team meetings also discuss teaching methodologies	10.7%	21.4%	53.6%	14.3%
JCSP team meetings plan cross-curricular work	21.4%	42.9%	21.4%	14.3%
JCSP team meetings review students' progress in achieving statements	42.9%	21.4%	17.9%	17.9%
Each student's attendance is reviewed at profiling meetings	39.3%	21.4%	25.0%	14.3%
Each student's punctuality is reviewed at profiling meetings	35.7%	25.0%	25.0%	14.3%
Each student's homework is reviewed at profiling meetings	35.7%	28.6%	25.0%	10.7%

Table 4.4   JCSP team meetings

Punctuality, attendance, homework and progress were reviewed during team meetings in nearly two-thirds of the schools evaluated, but teaching methods were discussed in fewer than one-third of them. The proportion of schools in which the number of profiling meetings is never adequate – nearly fifteen per cent – gives rise to concern. Similarly, the proportion of schools reporting that there is no discussion and review of important aspects of the programme at meetings is also of concern.

While communications between members of schools' JCSP teams were reported as being good in two-thirds of the schools visited, many programmes were reported to depend on informal meetings, which took place in the staff room, during tea breaks or in the corridors. While informal meetings are valuable, it is important that sufficient priority be given to holding regular formal planning meetings.

The following extracts from school inspection reports serve to illustrate the contrast in styles and effectiveness of JCSP teams in the schools evaluated.

> There is regular informal communication between JCSP teachers as well as monthly meetings, which all JCSP teachers are free to attend. The inspector attended an efficient and purposeful team meeting where the co-ordinator and nine others participated. These monthly meetings amount to ongoing review and planning, which is very valuable to the success of the programme.

This next quotation depicts what is, perhaps, a more widespread situation:

> There is regular informal communication between the JCSP co-ordinator and the teaching team. However, the potential for teamwork among teachers is not fully developed. There is evidence of a lack of clarity around team membership and the members of the team have varying views on the level and quality of existing teamwork.

All schools should give priority to ensuring regular communication among the JCSP team members. Also, where feasible, time should be made available for the team to discuss issues that are pertinent to the JCSP.

4.2.3   The JCSP Teaching Team

Table 4.5 identifies, according to questionnaire responses from JCSP co-ordinators, the factors that tend to influence the size of a JCSP teaching team in a school. It is evident from this table that the two principal factors influencing the size of this team were the availability of teachers, and the need for as many teachers as possible to have learning-support experience. It can be deduced from this, with some degree of certainty, that keeping the JCSP teaching team small is an important consideration for up to sixty-five per cent of schools, but not for the remainder. A small teaching team increases the likelihood of effective communications between members, and it also increases the likelihood of students developing a meaningful relationship with their teachers. Schools should keep their JCSP teaching teams reasonably small, but large enough to contain the range of skills required to provide an effective programme.

Factor	Very much	Somewhat	Slight	None
Availability of teachers	60.9%	26.1%	0	13.0%
As many teachers on team as possible with learning-support experience	56.5%	13.0%	13.0%	17.4%
Small team to aid communication and co-ordination	25.0%	40.0%	15.0%	20.0%
Large team to include as many teachers as possible	23.8%	9.5%	14.3%	52.4%

Table 4.5   Factors influencing the size of the JCSP teaching team

4.3   Co-ordination of the JCSP

Effective co-ordination is key to the success of the JCSP in a school. It is evident from the list of activities in Table 4.6 that the role of the co-ordinator is a demanding one, requiring insight and energy as well as organisational, interpersonal and administrative skills. Given that a great deal of the work of the co-ordinator is concerned with the establishment and running of a successful JCSP team, effective leadership skills are also important.

Activity	Proportion carrying out activity
Attending meetings of co-ordinators (JCSP Support Service)	100%
Developing and promoting cross-curricular integration	100%
Participating in continuous review of the programme	100%
Setting up and maintaining a system of student folders	100%
Assisting in the selection of profiling statements	100%
Maintenance of records in student profiling system	100%
Reporting to school staff on JCSP progress and development	96%
Development of JCSP initiatives in school	96%
Purchasing equipment and materials	93%
Liaising with parents	90%
Organising and chairing meetings of JCSP team	90%
Working with HSCL teacher	73%
Management of school budget for the JCSP	61%
Monitoring attendance	60%
Dealing with behavioural issues	60%

Table 4.6   Activities undertaken by JCSP co-ordinators

An important aspect of the co-ordinator's role that emerged from inspectors' reports was their commitment to the welfare and progress of the students in their care. As one inspector commented:

> The co-ordinator accommodates effectively students experiencing learning difficulties, is committed to the aims of the JCSP and manages the programme with energy and diligence. The leadership of the co-ordinator is crucial to the ongoing promotion and expansion of the programme.

Many co-ordinators, when interviewed as part of the evaluation, placed planning issues and the profiling of students high on their list of priorities. As outlined previously, these issues require regular businesslike meetings with other JCSP team members to address them effectively. Keeping accurate and up-to-date records is another important aspect of the work of the co-ordinator. Plans of work also need to be drawn up, team decisions need to be recorded and student profiles need to be regularly updated.

Co-ordinators were asked to state the kinds of JCSP records they keep; responses are tabulated in Table 4.7. As can be seen, not all co-ordinators kept records of the profiling statements being worked on by students. Similarly, twenty-four per cent of all co-ordinators did not keep minutes of JCSP team meetings.

Type of record	Proportion of co-ordinators
Statements completed	92.9%
Statements being worked on	85.7%
The school's JCSP	77.8%
Minutes of JCSP team meetings	76.0%
Student assessment records	70.8%
Communications with parents	63.0%
Communications with the Department of Education and Science	50.0%
Attendance records of students	48.1%
JCSP budget and accounts	33.3%

Table 4.7   Records kept by the JCSP co-ordinator

The evaluation found that there was wide variation in the scope and quality of records kept by schools. Seven schools were reported to have appropriate record-keeping systems. In a further eighteen the administration of JCSP records and paperwork was described as being "reasonable" or "fair", while the remaining five schools visited were reported to have "poor" record-keeping, or none at all.

Given this finding, it is recommended that schools, with the aid of the JCSP Support Service, plan and implement appropriate systems for the preparation, storage, updating and retention of JCSP records. Use should be made of ICT to the greatest extent possible in this work.

Table 4.8 gives an indication of the resources schools made available to JCSP co-ordinators. While most reported having access to a phone, computer and photocopier, the relatively low proportion (60.7%) that reported having a dedicated office may reduce the effectiveness of these resources.

Resource	Proportion of co-ordinators
Photocopier	93.1%
Computer and printer	93.1%
Phone	90.0%
E-mail and internet	88.9%
Office	60.7%

Table 4.8   Resources available to the JCSP co-ordinator

In general it was found that the amount of time allocated to JCSP co-ordination varied from one to four hours per week, with half of the schools evaluated allocating two hours or less. The issue of inadequate time for co-ordination, including the profiling of students, was raised repeatedly in the course of the evaluation. Only forty-one per cent of co-ordinators agreed that adequate time was allowed for the co-ordination of the programme in their school. Other difficulties encountered by co-ordinators included balancing co-ordination duties with other responsibilities within the school, difficulties with timetabling lessons for students, and a lack of time for organising or attending team meetings, as well as time for paperwork and administration. In order to improve the situation co-ordinators suggested that there should be more flexibility in timetabling and a greater allocation of time by the Department of Education and Science for planning. It was also suggested by co-ordinators that a JCSP folder review period should be timetabled each week, and that JCSP teachers should be allocated more time for meetings.

The following quotations from inspection reports illustrate the range and quality of co-ordination found in schools:

> The co-ordinator has a large degree of delegated responsibility for the running of all aspects of the programme. The dovetailing of the different subjects of the cross-curricular components of the programme is particularly well managed. The co-ordinator has excellently combined the management, communication and teaching functions of the role to deliver a very good programme, close to the ideals of JCSP.

In contrast:

> The co-ordinator has a time allocation of two hours and forty minutes for the work of co-ordination, but regards this time as inadequate to allow for the satisfactory execution of the duties. Consequently there is not much documentation available in the school to indicate decisions or plans emanating from meetings.

For the most part, co-ordination of the JCSP in schools is carried out in an effective manner. Areas that need to be addressed include record-keeping and provision for more frequent meetings of the JCSP team. In three schools, inspectors found that there was a significant deficiency in the time allocated to co-ordination of the JCSP. This particular issue gives rise to concern, particularly in light of the 0.25 WTE allocation to schools per forty-five students enrolled on the programme.

It was clear that the difficulties experienced by co-ordinators as a result of the lack of co-ordination time were exacerbated as the number of students in a school enrolled on the JCSP increased. Where large numbers of students were following the programme there was a serious impact on the time requirements for profiling, meetings and record-keeping. In light of these findings it is recommended that schools should carefully select students for the programme. This should involve recording the criteria that determine each student's selection, stating how the JCSP is appropriate in meeting the needs of each student. These records should be retained in the school. Further issues concerning the selection of students for participation in the programme are explored in Chapter 6.

4.4   Class grouping, timetabling and subject choice

4.4.1   Organisation and timetabling of classes

The manner in which class groups are organised, and the considerations taken into account when timetabling these groups, are important determinants of the JCSP experience for students. In the majority of schools included in this evaluation, JCSP students constituted a separate class group in each year. In two mainstream schools the JCSP class in first year comprised the entire first-year student intake, and it was clearly intended that this would prevail into the students' second and third years. A situation such as this raises questions with regard to the application by schools of appropriate selection criteria for the programme. It also makes the task of co-ordination more difficult.

In response to a question regarding the considerations that affect timetabling for the JCSP, more than sixty per cent of co-ordinators stated that there was a necessity to provide additional time for Mathematics and English. However, more than sixty per cent also stated that the need to have lessons in Mathematics and English timetabled in the morning was either not a consideration, or was only slightly considered. Given the central importance of literacy and numeracy in the JCSP, it is recommended that schools give priority to timetabling English and Mathematics lessons in the morning as much as possible. Students tend to succeed better at those subjects that require a high degree of concentration if they have these lessons in the earlier part of the day.

Although JCSP students formed a separate class group in most schools, in some schools they took a number of their subjects within mainstream (non-JCSP) Junior Certificate classes. This practice can have beneficial effects in integrating JCSP students in the overall junior cycle cohort and it also allows for a wider range of subjects to be taken by students. Operating mixed class groups – those with both JCSP and mainstream Junior Certificate students – calls for effective planning and organisation on the part of teachers. Also, with a separate JCSP class group a teacher can often teach more than one subject to such a group, and this can help in establishing continuity and support in a range of subjects.

Table 4.9 gives an indication of the number of teachers JCSP classes met in any one week in those schools evaluated. From this it can be seen that over half the JCSP classes in the schools that participated in this evaluation met ten or more different teachers each week.

Year	Number of different teachers met each week	Proportion of classes
1	3–9	38.5%
1	10–13	38.5%
1	14+	23%
2	3–9	42.3%
2	10–13	46.2%
2	14+	11.5%
3	3–9	46.2%
3	10–13	42.3%
3	14+	11.5%

Table 4.9   Proportion of classes and number of teachers per class in each year of the JCSP

Keeping the JCSP teaching team as small as practicable is in the best interests of meeting the aims of the programme. Students find it easier to relate to a smaller number of teachers and communications among teachers can be more easily facilitated. With a small teaching team there is more time for high quality relationships to be formed between students and teachers. Large JCSP teaching teams may sometimes reflect a low priority being attached to JCSP classes by school managements. It is recommended that schools give priority to reducing the number of teachers met by individual JCSP class groups.

4.4.2   Subject choice and the selection of profiling statements

From inspection reports it is clear that in the majority of schools the same group that undertakes the overall planning for the JCSP are also involved in selecting subjects for JCSP classes. When the profiling statements to be achieved by students in each subject are selected the most characteristic element of the JCSP comes into operation. The curriculum is mediated to students through the profiling system (described in section 2.5) and it is through this system that the JCSP focuses on the individual student and his/her needs. It is through this system also that subjects are linked and a cross-curricular element introduced. In this way, profiling provides a context and a tool for co-operation between teachers.

It was found that in about two-thirds of the schools involved in the evaluation subject teachers selected profiling statements for their own classes. In a minority of instances the selection of statements for student profiling was made by the JCSP planning team and then implemented by the subject teachers. In an even smaller number of instances students made the selection, but where this happened, it took place in co-operation with the subject teacher. It was the practice in fifteen per cent of schools visited that all students in a class group were always assigned similar statements, regardless of individual ability. In a small number of schools students seemed unaware of the purpose and use of profiling statements. It is clear that wide variation in the practice of student profiling exists in schools.

To involve students more effectively in their own learning, and to provide realisable short-term targets for their work, profiling statements should be used to the greatest extent possible within the JCSP. It is recommended, therefore, that the selection and assessment of statements be co-ordinated within a school, that students be involved to the greatest extent possible in the selection and assessment of their statements, and that the selection of statements should take individual differences into account.

It is evident from the comments of co-ordinators and subject teachers in their questionnaire responses that while the system of profiling of students has clear benefits, and indeed is central to the JCSP, it is not without its problems. These relate principally to the administrative workload associated with, and the time demands of, the process. Other difficulties, as referred to in inspectors' reports, arise from the fact that not all teachers implement profiling.

Appropriate training, with a focus on the benefits of ICT, that would enable co-ordinators and teachers to implement profiling more efficiently, should be considered. The JCSP profiling system would also benefit from a review at national level, particularly with a view to reducing the administrative burden on schools, especially that on co-ordinators and teachers.

4.5 Programme Review

One of the reasons why a school should review its own JCSP is to ensure that the programme continues to meet the identified needs of its students. Ideally, therefore, the JCSP should be subjected to regular informal and formal review.

The JCSP can be kept under continual informal review through asking such questions as:

What is working well?

What could be improved?

What more needs to be done?

Towards the end of each school year the outcomes of such informal review could be documented, and this would inform planning for the succeeding year.

An internal formal review of the JCSP should involve obtaining the views of teachers, students and parents through the use of surveys or through meeting with these various groups. Such a formal review need only take place every three to four years. In more than two-thirds of the schools visited by inspectors it was considered that the JCSP needed a formal review involving teachers, students, and parents.

In some schools it was found that meetings to carry out student profiling sometimes doubled up as meetings to review the programme. In most cases, however, separate review meetings were held, generally once a year, but sometimes more frequently.

In general it was found that the JCSP co-ordinator participated in all JCSP review meetings, while the JCSP team took part in practically all of them. The school principal and subject teachers participated in more than half of the reviews undertaken, as did specialist teachers (such as the guidance counsellor, HSCL teacher, etc.). In some instances, where the review took place in a general or special staff meeting, the whole teaching staff contributed.

It is recommended that all schools should keep the JCSP under continual informal review involving as many members of the JCSP staff as possible, with a more formal review of the programme taking place every three to four years. The outcomes of such internal reviews should inform planning for the future development of the programme.

4.6   Summary of findings and recommendations

4.6.1   Findings

The following is a summary of the main findings in relation to the organisation of the JCSP in those schools that participated in this evaluation.

- The frequency of JCSP team meetings in schools varies considerably: approximately twenty per cent of schools held no JCSP meetings during the school year.
- The majority of JCSP schools do not have appropriate record-keeping systems in place.
- The large size of the teaching team in the majority of schools is not in accordance with guidelines on JCSP and may not be in the best interest of the programme.
- There is wide variation in schools regarding the practice of student profiling. In most schools there was little involvement by students in the process.
- The student profiling system makes considerable time and administration demands on schools.
- For most schools the necessity to provide JCSP students with additional teaching time in Mathematics and English is an important consideration.
- While there is a good level of informal review of the JCSP in schools formal review of the programme takes place in only a minority of schools.

4.6.2   Recommendations

The following recommendations are made with regard to the organisation of the JCSP in schools.

Recommendations for schools

- All schools should have a JCSP planning group that includes the principal, the JCSP co-ordinator, and representatives of the school's JCSP teaching team. Planning for the programme in a school should include curriculum, assessment, resources, student selection and staffing. Schools should also allocate time for meetings to plan and run the JCSP. Each school should document its JCSP.
- Schools should ensure that formal and informal reviews takes place so as to ensure that the programme continues to meet the needs of students.
- Schools, with the aid of the support service where necessary, should plan and implement systems, including the use of ICT, for the preparation, storage, updating and retention of JCSP records.

- Schools should keep their JCSP teaching teams as small as practicable, consistent with having enough team members with the range of skills necessary to provide an effective programme.
- Mathematics and English lessons should be timetabled, as far as possible, in the morning so as to enhance the effectiveness of the provision for literacy and numeracy within the JCSP.
- Profiling should be implemented in each school's JCSP. The selection and assessment of profiling statements should be co-ordinated and student involvement should be facilitated.
- Each school's JCSP criteria for selection of students should be documented. Records should indicate how each student is expected to benefit from the JCSP and these should be retained in the school.

Recommendations for policy-makers and policy advisers

- The JCSP student profiling system should be subjected to a thorough review with a view to exploring ways of reducing the administrative requirement of the programme on schools. Training should be provided to enable co-ordinators and teachers to implement profiling efficiently through an increased use of ICT, including the development of suitable software for this purpose.

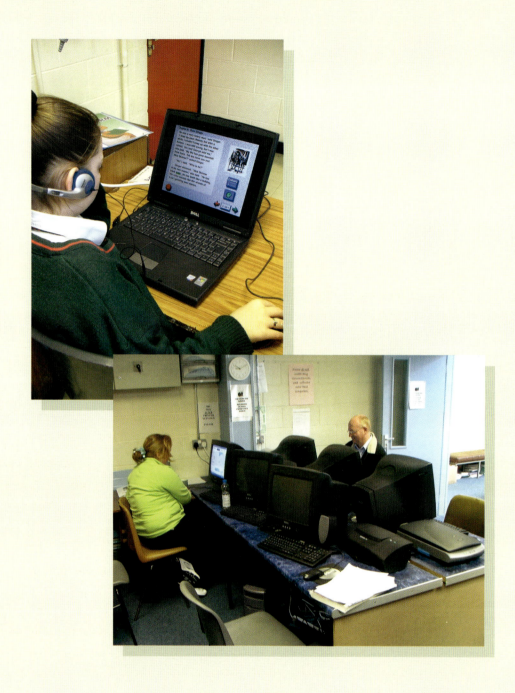

5 Supporting the JCSP
Resources

5.1 Introduction

This chapter examines how schools use the additional resources provided by the Department of Education and Science to JCSP schools, and the views of schools on the adequacy of these resources. An analysis of the take-up and organisation of in-career professional development associated with the JCSP is also included.

5.2 Schools' resources for the JCSP

The extra resources provided to schools for JCSP purposes by the Department of Education and Science include an additional teaching time allocation and additional *per capita* funding.

5.2.1 Use of additional teaching time allocation

As mentioned in section 2.6, the additional teaching time allocation to a school in respect of the JCSP amounts to 0.25 of a teacher, or 5.5 hours per week, per group of forty-five students participating in the programme. In twenty-one of the thirty schools evaluated one to four hours per week was allocated for JCSP co-ordination duties. This time was used for planning and administration work, record-keeping, staff meetings, and meetings with students and parents. Twenty-five of the schools used the balance of the additional time allocation to reduce class sizes, or to increase the time allocated to co-ordination work and learning support. The following extract from an inspection report illustrates how one school used its additional teaching time:

> Additional teaching time is used as much as possible to split classes so that generally each class contains ten to twelve students … The additional JCSP time allocation is used for the co-ordinator and for extra teaching support. The co-ordinator has six hours allocated for co-ordination of activities – four of these are from the JCSP allocation and two from the school.

In some schools co-ordination time was shared with time that was allocated for other purposes in schools. Where there was an overlap of roles, for example, where the JCSP co-ordinator was also the guidance counsellor, or had time available from an assistant principal post, it was sometimes unclear as to which time allocation was being used for co-ordination of the programme. In some of these instances inspectors reported that it would not have been necessary to "borrow" further co-ordination time from other sources if the initial allocation of time for the JCSP had been used appropriately.

Just over half the JCSP co-ordinators surveyed considered that their time allocation for co-ordinating the programme was inadequate. This was especially so in schools that had large numbers of students enrolled in the programme. (This issue is also treated in section 4.3 in the context of the co-ordination of the JCSP in schools). The fact that the issue of co-ordination time as a resource is a major problem, particularly for schools with large numbers of JCSP students, suggests that such schools should become focused in their selection of students for the programme.

Given the significant workload involved in co-ordinating the JCSP, particularly in those schools where large numbers of JCSP students are enrolled, consideration should be given to revising the additional whole-time teacher equivalent allocation currently made available to schools. As student numbers increase so too does the administrative workload on schools.

Special schools do not receive any additional teaching time allocation for the JCSP. Given that co-ordination is such an important aspect of implementing the JCSP, and that the majority of mainstream schools typically use between two and four hours per week of the department's teaching time allocation for co-ordination purposes, it seems inappropriate that special schools do not receive any additional teaching time allocation. Consideration needs to be given to providing such schools with some additional allocation of teaching time. Overall, the numbers of students taking the JCSP in special schools are small, with consequent small class sizes.

5.2.2 Use of JCSP funding

Each school providing the JCSP receives a once-off *per capita* grant from the Department of Education and Science for each student entering the programme[5]. From inspectors' reports, and from the questionnaire responses of co-ordinators, it is apparent that this grant allocation does not adequately cover all the activities, materials or projects that the programme can offer students. Two-thirds of co-ordinators, for example, stated that the existing resources for the JCSP in their school were not adequate. Table 5.1 indicates how those schools that participated in the evaluation spend funds on the JCSP.

Category	Proportion of schools
Books and reading materials	81%
Class materials and resources	81%
Outdoor education, field-work, trips, and transport provision	76%
Awards and celebrations	71%
Folders and stationery	71%
Software	29%
IT equipment	24%

Table 5.1   How schools spend funds on the JCSP

Other areas in which funds were spent included various competitions and activities, such as the Readalong, Make-a-Book and Fusebox[6] projects, paired-reading initiatives, open days or evenings for parents, calculators for students, newsletters, photocopying, drama workshops, homework clubs, staff development and visiting speakers. An example of how funds are used is given in the following extract from one school report:

---

5 At the time of this evaluation the grant allocation was €63.49 per student and was in addition to regular student capitation funding. This grant has remained unchanged since the JCSP was launched in 1996.

6 Fusebox is a music education programme funded by the JCSP Support Service. The programme originated in 2001/2002 as a community initiative, operated by Fusebox, and was built around a series of workshops during which students from different schools composed a musical piece that was then professionally recorded. The JCSP Support Service succeeded in offering the programme to a wider range of schools.

The financial resources provided are well expended on materials and events for the JCSP. The largest expenditure is on awards and celebrations, which are regarded by the school as a good investment. Money is also spent on classroom materials and resources, and a smaller amount on trips and outings.

It was found that schools tended to acquire funds from other sources to assist in the running of their JCSP. Schools, for example, made use of SCP and Disadvantaged Areas Scheme (DAS) funding to assist in running their JCSP. In other instances the local VEC had provided funding, or learning-support funds were utilised. Fund-raising activities were also organised by parents, teachers, and students. The following extract from one inspection report illustrates how one school funded the programme:

The money provided for the JCSP as such is not adequate to fund all the activities and resources required, and monies from the SCP and from the VEC are used to cover the balance. For example, music classes, use of swimming pool and … are financed from other sources.

Co-ordinators were asked to describe their level of access to JCSP funding and resources within their school. From Table 5.2 it is clear that, in most schools evaluated, co-ordinators usually control, or have ready access to, funding and resources for the programme.

Nature of access	Always	Usually	Sometime	Never
Co-ordinator decides on allocation of JCSP funding	37.0%	33.3%	7.4%	22.2%
Resources are provided on request to JCSP co-ordinator	36.7%	56.7%	6.7%	0
Co-ordinator can quickly obtain access to resources when required	36.7%	43.3%	20.0%	0

Table 5.2　Access by co-ordinators to resources for the JCSP

Table 5.3 lists the deficits, according to co-ordinators, in the JCSP as a result of inadequate resourcing.

Deficit as a result of lack of resources	Proportion of co-ordinators
Too few teachers[7]	41%
Inadequate equipment or resources	29%
Difficulty obtaining access to resources within school	6%
Insufficient co-ordination planning time	6%
Insufficient teacher planning time	6%
Need for JCSP storage room	6%
Inadequate provision for students with behavioural difficulties	6%

Table 5.3　Co-ordinators' perception of deficits in the JCSP as a result of lack of funding

---

7　JCSP co-ordinators expressed the view that with greater funding some class sizes could be reduced further through the employment of additional teachers.

The following extract from an inspection report summarises succinctly the difficulties for schools in resourcing the JCSP.

> Finance made available to the school for JCSP is fully expended on JCSP needs. Other needs of JCSP are supplied from within the school, or from other programmes in operation in the school. Funds are raised within the school, but it is clear that the monies provided do not go very far in financing the JCSP in the school. After one year, finance became tight and is a constant cause of concern.

The current *per capita* grant from the Department of Education and Science for schools in respect of the JCSP appears inadequate on it own. However, schools can, and many do, use elements of funding made available for other Department of Education and Science initiatives to support their JCSP, such as SCP and DAS funding. The funding arrangements currently in place for the JCSP should be reviewed. Its funding should be considered in light of funding made available for other initiatives and programmes in schools.

5.3 In-career development (ICD)

The area of in-career professional development for JCSP teachers was explored as part of the evaluation. Three main issues arose in this area:
- the take-up of ICD by JCSP personnel
- the organisation of JCSP-related ICD
- the identification of ICD needs by JCSP school personnel.

5.3.1 Take-up of ICD by JCSP school personnel

Management in more than half the schools evaluated reported having encouraged and facilitated attendance at ICD by JCSP personnel. Notwithstanding this, close to one-third of these schools, according to inspectors' reports, never participated in any JCSP in-career development courses. Further, in a third of the schools evaluated, the JCSP co-ordinators were the only member of staff to have participated in ICD. With regard to twelve schools in particular, inspectors recommended that JCSP teachers be facilitated with more ICD.

Table 5.4 shows the extent of the engagement of a range of JCSP school personnel with ICD courses in the two years previous to the evaluation.

Number of in-career development courses attended	Proportion responding who attended JCSP in-career development in the previous two years				
	0	1	2	3	4
JCSP co-ordinators (n = 24)[8]	17%	25%	25%	21%	12%
Resource teachers (n = 7)	70%	13%	0	17%	0
Learning-support teachers (n = 17)	41%	29%	12%	18%	0
Guidance counsellors (n = 2)	0	100%	0	0	0
Subject teachers (n = 160)	69%	18%	9%	2%	3%

Table 5.4 ICD taken in the 2000/2001 and 2001/2002 school years

---

8 It is likely that virtually all JCSP co-ordinators had attended co-ordinators meetings, but some may not have included these as ICD courses.

While the JCSP Support Service has provided a wide range of ICD since the programme was launched in 1996[9] it is a matter of concern that a large proportion of JCSP personnel have not availed of any JCSP related ICD, and of those who have, few have attended more than one such course.

In general, while teachers considered ICD courses to be helpful, the most successful courses included those that brought co-ordinators together, those concerned with transfer programmes and courses on specific skills. The specific skills courses were particularly useful, according to one co-ordinator, because they were *"directly transferable to the classroom and could have an immediate impact and benefit"*.

Given the low take-up among JCSP school personnel of relevant ICD, it is recommended that schools should assess staff needs and, in turn, plan for appropriate participation in JCSP ICD as part of their development planning process.

5.3.2   Organisation of ICD courses

In their reports inspectors made reference to the difficulties experienced by some teachers in accessing relevant ICD courses. It was evident that the majority of courses attended by JCSP personnel were Dublin based and frequently the amount of travel necessary to attend these courses was described as being excessive. An inspector's observation on ICD issues pertaining to a school far from Dublin emphasised the problem:

> Staff in this school have had very little in-career development for JCSP, and most of them expressed the need for more subject-specific in-service, ideally delivered locally, or at least regionally. They would benefit greatly from training in profiling, cross-curricular literacy work and active learning methodologies.

When asked to make suggestions regarding the organisation of JCSP-related ICD, co-ordinators regularly sought more local or regional provision. In this context, a strong demand was registered for more courses to be provided outside the Dublin area, particularly in the west and north-west. Co-ordinators also preferred the idea of having in-school ICD courses for JCSP teams, as well as courses out of school time, at weekends or at the beginning or end of a school term. Co-ordinators also referred to the desirability of increasing links between JCSP schools in an area (for example, clusters of schools) with induction and repeated ICD courses for teachers new to the JCSP. It could be argued, however, with regard to the induction of teachers new to the programme that schools that have been providing the programme for two years or more should be able to provide their own induction programmes, with a minimal contribution from the relevant support service.

Overall, the JCSP Support Service should undertake a review of the strategies employed in the delivery of ICD provision associated with the programme. It is clear that face-to-face courses delivered at central venues are not always the most appropriate mode of delivery.

5.3.3   Identified in-career development needs

Teachers generally expressed a high degree of satisfaction with the quality of the in-career development provided by the support service. When asked to identify their ICD needs all teachers associated with the JCSP put forward a wide range of suggestions. In the case of JCSP

---

9   See Appendix 3 for details of ICD courses provided by the JCSP Support Service between 1996 and 2003.

subject teachers, for example, while they suggested many courses that were subject specific in nature, they also suggested a wide range of generic type courses on teaching and learning. Among those identified were courses on:

- teaching students with reading, writing or numeracy difficulties
- teaching students with special educational needs, including attention-deficit hyperactivity disorder (ADHD), dyslexia and deafness
- discipline and behavioural management
- cross-curricular approaches to learning
- whole-school approaches to the JCSP
- ICT

Subject teachers also emphasised the need for courses on effective methods for teaching JCSP students, and for cluster meetings of subject teachers. Nine per cent of JCSP subject teachers referred to a need for ICD courses on special-needs topics. In many instances, these courses of a generic nature were already being provided by the support service.

Resource teachers emphasised their need for courses that would provide them with information on equipment and resources for the JCSP. They also stated that support was needed in relation to the role that resource teachers can play in the JCSP. In-career development courses suggested by learning-support teachers included whole-school approaches to literacy, literacy throughout the curriculum, and special needs and specific learning difficulties in the JCSP. Learning-support teachers also mentioned a need for JCSP subject-specific ICD courses, particularly in the areas of technology education – Metalwork and Materials Technology (Wood), as well as CSPE, SPHE and Science. These teachers also referred to specialised courses related to special educational needs, including autism, emotional and behavioural disorders, Asperger's syndrome and ADHD. Guidance counsellors suggested a need for ICD courses that related to ways of exploring fully the needs of students, and to career options for students and best practice in guidance for JCSP students.

When planning future ICD programmes for JCSP teachers the support service should ensure provision of subject specific courses, but also generic courses on teaching and learning. Also, the provision of more ICD courses in the area of special educational needs should to be addressed.

5.4 Summary of findings and recommendations

5.4.1 Findings

The following is a summary of the main findings in relation to how schools employ resources made available for the JCSP by the Department of Education and Science.

- Appropriate co-ordination is necessary for the effective implementation of the JCSP. Schools typically use between two and four hours a week of the additional teaching time allocation for JCSP co-ordination activities. Difficulties arise in co-ordination when there is an inappropriate allocation of co-ordination time. It was found that difficulties in the co-ordination of the programme and the profiling of students were exacerbated as the number of students in the JCSP increased.
- It is the view of JCSP co-ordinators that the funds provided for the programme by the Department of Education and Science do not adequately meet the needs of providing an effective JCSP in a school. For most schools this funding is supplemented by funds from other sources.

- A low proportion of JCSP personnel, other than co-ordinators, participated in relevant ICD courses in the two years prior to this evaluation. Of those who did participate, there was a high degree of satisfaction with the quality of the courses attended.
- Some schools experience difficulty in accessing relevant ICD courses.

5.4.2 Recommendations

The following recommendations are made with regard to the implementation of JCSP resources made available to schools.

Recommendations for schools

- Where programmes with similar objectives to those of the JCSP operate in a school, such as the SCP, the school should ensure that such programmes are co-ordinated with the JCSP so as to maximise the benefits to students.
- Schools should assess staff needs, and in turn plan for appropriate participation in relevant JCSP in-career development courses as part of their development planning process.

Recommendations for policy-makers and policy advisers

- At present an additional allocation of 0.25 teachers (or 5.5 hours per week) for each forty-five students enrolled is provided to schools. Given the significant workload involved in co-ordinating the JCSP, particularly in those schools where large numbers of JCSP students are enrolled, consideration should be given to revising the additional whole-time teacher equivalent allocation currently made available to schools.
- Consideration needs to be given to providing special schools with some additional allocation of teaching time.
- The funding arrangements currently in place for the JCSP should be reviewed and should be considered in light of funding made available for other initiatives and programmes in schools.
- The JCSP Support Service should undertake a review of the strategies employed in the delivery of ICD provision associated with the programme. There is also a need for more in-career development courses in the area of special educational needs.

6 Who Takes the JCSP, and Why?
Student Selection Procedures

6.1 Introduction

This chapter examines the criteria and procedures that schools apply when selecting students for the JCSP. It will be seen that schools have adopted varying approaches when selecting students for the programme, approaches that can involve school personnel visiting primary schools as well as the homes of prospective students, the holding of open days or information meetings for parents, and administration of different student assessment procedures. The wide range of school personnel that can be involved in the student selection process for the JCSP will be shown. The chapter concludes with a review of selection issues relating to students with special educational needs.

6.2 Criteria used for selecting students for the JCSP

While the JCSP is particularly aimed at students who are at risk of early school leaving, many schools also consider the programme to be suitable for students with special educational needs. This issue is addressed in section 6.5. Examples of indicators of early school leaving, as discussed in section 2.3, include under-achievement and low academic performance, problems in students' homes, and absenteeism.

The majority of schools that participated in this evaluation assessed incoming students and, on this basis, placed those who displayed poor levels of attainment or specific learning difficulties in JCSP classes. As one inspection report commented:

> Informal contacts are made with the primary school teachers ... The students undertake assessment tests ... A group of twenty students is selected and their parents are contacted in writing ... The parents are invited to an interview where the benefits of the JCSP are outlined. From this group sixteen students are offered a place on the JCSP.

In essence, it was found that academic attainment, as reflected in students' assessment results on entry to post-primary school, is the principal criterion by which most schools select students for the JCSP.

In just over one-third of schools evaluated inspectors stated that recognised indicators of risk of early school leaving, other than assessment results, were taken into account in forming JCSP classes. In some of these schools consultation with other personnel (e.g., SCP personnel) also informed the selection process. Another inspection report commented:

> The focus is on students at risk, poor attendees, those with literacy problems and special needs and those receiving learning support. The criterion applied when determining whether or not an individual is potentially in need of the JCSP is encapsulated in the question "will this student be able to follow the Junior Certificate [curriculum] successfully in a large number of subjects, without support?"

From inspector's reports, however, it is clear that many schools do not consider the wide range of indicators of early school leaving when selecting students for the JCSP. Schools' selection criteria should be broadened, and this is particularly important for those schools that attach more weight to students' assessment results than any other indicators.

6.3 Procedures used for selecting students for the JCSP

Just as schools differed regarding the criteria that they used for selecting students for the programme, differences were also found to exist with regard to the timing of selection procedures, the extent of contact between parents and feeder primary schools, and the type of student assessments administered. The selection process frequently involved visits to students' homes and their primary schools, and holding meetings or open days for parents and students, as well as the assessment of students. It was particularly apparent from inspectors' reports that in many second-level schools there was a considerable amount of collaboration with feeder primary schools with regard to selecting students for participation in the JCSP. A systematic follow-up to the initial selection of students is implemented in some schools and this is discussed in section 6.3.4.

6.3.1 Visits to primary schools and students' homes

It was found that in almost one-third of the schools evaluated staff members visited local primary schools, and in some instances information packs on the school and the JCSP were distributed. In some schools, parents were also involved in the selection process by means of visits by staff members to the homes of potential JCSP students in the year before entry. The guidance counsellor, the school principal or, where available, the HSCL co-ordinator, generally undertook such visits. JCSP schools found these visits to be valuable in helping to establish the needs of, and the supports required for students. They also contributed to creating an awareness of the JCSP among primary schools, which helped with the selection process.

The involvement of primary schools and parents in the selection of students enhances the reliability of the selection process and contributes to the development of a strong bond between the home and the school. It is a practice that should be adopted by all schools providing the JCSP.

6.3.2 Informing parents about the JCSP

Open days or information meetings for the parents of incoming first-year students were held annually by several of the schools evaluated. The overriding aim of these events was to impart information about the school and, in particular, the JCSP. Primary schools were sometimes involved in the organisation of such events. This is summarised in the following quotation from one inspection report:

> The school makes an initial contact with parents by having an information-giving presentation in a local primary school or community centre. A brief explanation of the goals of JCSP is given and this is supported with examples of project work and photographs of in and out-of-school activities. There is an emphasis on the positive role parents can play in enhancing the success of their child in the post-primary school …

These events assist in establishing links with parents, and they also help in the selection process by providing second-level schools with information on the needs of incoming students.

6.3.3   Assessing students

Up to three-quarters of the schools that participated in the evaluation made use of specific assessment instruments to assess incoming first-year students. Of the remaining schools, some had an "automatic" transfer of a group of students from a local feeder primary school because of local conditions, while others, having too few students to make up more than one first-year group, made the whole year group into a JCSP class. Students in the special schools included in the evaluation were selected to follow the JCSP on the grounds that they could benefit from the programme.

There was a wide range of practices among schools with regard to the assessment of students as part of the selection process for the JCSP. Many, for example, used several different assessment instruments, which included a wide range of commercially-produced tests (e.g., Drumcondra Reasoning Test, AH2/3/4, Nelson Non-Verbal Reasoning Tests and Young Group Reading Test). Of those schools evaluated, half used both literacy and numeracy tests. A small number employed literacy tests only, while fewer than half used either verbal or non-verbal reasoning or general intelligence tests. It was found that a quarter of the schools evaluated had strong liaison with their feeder primary schools, which involved collaborative work on assessing students before they entered second level.

In those schools that streamed students on the basis of assessment results it was found that those with the lowest scores constituted the JCSP classes. In other schools the assessments were followed by interviews, meetings of teachers to discuss results, or reviews of psychological assessment results. Local conditions and specific situations sometimes led to different approaches, for example:

> There is no entrance examination for the students. [They] are placed in class groups depending on the primary school they attended. After six weeks, assessment tests are given in every subject by the class teachers. Screening tests in numeracy and literacy are administered. Cognisance is taken of reports from the primary schools … They are then placed in groups according to the streaming system.

While the assessment of students before entry to post-primary schools is an established practice, the range of assessment instruments being used gives rise to some concern. It is questionable, for example, whether they are all appropriate for identifying students who would benefit from the JCSP. It is important, therefore, that assessment instruments used by schools are norm-referenced, culturally fair and up-to-date.

It is recommended that the JCSP Support Service, in collaboration with the National Educational Psychological Service (NEPS), should develop and circulate appropriate guidelines to schools on best practice for the selection of students for the JCSP. This should include advice on the kinds of assessment instruments that should be used as part of any selection procedures.

6.3.4   Follow-up to selection

In a number of schools there was follow-up to the initial assessment used for selection purposes. In response to their questionnaire, for example, almost three-quarters of learning-support teachers stated that all students were assessed again following their enrolment in the JCSP. This follow-up ranged from regular to occasional assessment of students. Such follow-up, and action resulting from follow-up, is required so that all students who might benefit from the JCSP can continue to participate in the programme, while those who might no longer require the support of the JCSP can be identified and provided with the opportunity to follow the mainstream Junior Certificate programme.

6.4   Personnel involved in the student selection process

Table 6.1 gives a summary of the school personnel involved in selecting students for the JCSP each year. It is based on responses to the various questionnaires issued as part of the evaluation, and on school inspection reports. It shows that a wide range of personnel are involved in this process. What is surprising is that only half the JCSP co-ordinators have an involvement in the selection of students.

Category	Proportion of respondents involved in identifying and selecting students for the JCSP
Guidance counsellor	74%
Learning-support teacher	73%
Principal or deputy principal	60%
Resource teacher	56%
SCP co-ordinator	55%
JCSP co-ordinator	50%
HSCL teacher	36%
Subject teacher	24%

Table 6.1   Personnel with an involvement in the identification and selection of students for the JCSP

It is common practice that the school principal, perhaps in collaboration with the HSCL teacher or the guidance counsellor, or both, will select the students who will form an incoming JCSP class. Typically, the principal arranges visits to the local primary schools, and the HSCL co-ordinator and guidance counsellor carry out the assessment and selection. In one well-developed selection system the process was described as follows:

> The principal conducts visits to the local primary schools, where an awareness of the JCSP has been fostered effectively by such interface. As a result, principals of the feeder primary schools have been pro-active in identifying students who would benefit from JCSP … and in advising the [second-level] principal of the needs of the individuals concerned … The [second-level] school is active in promoting an awareness among parents of the benefits of the programme … for students at risk of early school leaving … Standardised literacy and numeracy tests are utilised to identify student achievement.

In those schools that had a HSCL teacher, they usually met with teachers of sixth-class students, as well as with parents of potential JCSP students to explain the value of the JCSP. In response to their questionnaire, for example, sixty-eight per cent of HSCL teachers stated that they had contact with parents regarding the possible enrolment of children in the JCSP. In general, the nature of the contact involved talking to parents about the programme, either informally during home visits or in feeder primary schools. In their responses, HSCL teachers suggested that the selection process for students for the JCSP would be improved by having greater consultation with the primary schools and with parents. They also stated that more clearly defined student selection policies in post-primary schools with regard to the JCSP would be helpful.

In schools which were part of the SCP it was not uncommon that the SCP co-ordinators were involved in the selection of students. This usually happened through meetings of the SCP co-ordinator with primary school teachers, or through assisting in the transfer programme from primary to post-primary. Almost one-third of SCP co-ordinators who responded to the questionnaire also stated that they had contact with parents regarding the possible enrolment of students in the JCSP.

Inspection reports recommended involving a greater range of school personnel in identifying and selecting students for the JCSP, wherever this was not already the case. It was evident that not all schools had contact with the parents of incoming JCSP students. Schools should involve parents in the selection process. Further, it is considered important for consistency between the selection process and the teaching of the programme that the JCSP co-ordinator be involved in the selection of students.

6.5 The JCSP and students with special educational needs

Many schools consider the JCSP to be suitable for students with special educational needs. Practically all JCSP co-ordinators surveyed, for example, stated that there were students with special educational needs in their JCSP classes. Table 6.2 shows the range of special educational needs of the students in the thirty schools evaluated.

Category of special educational need	Number of schools responding to question	Proportion of schools responding with students in that category
Learning disability (mild, moderate, severe)	29	97%
Emotional or behavioural disorder	29	97%
Specific learning disability	29	90%
Speech or language disorder	29	72%
Physical disability	28	39%
Sensory impairment	27	33%
Multiple disability	28	32%
Autism or autistic spectrum disorder	28	25%

Table 6.2 Students with special educational needs and the JCSP

Two of the schools that participated in the evaluation were special schools. In these schools it was found that all the students in the senior section that were considered capable of benefiting from the JCSP were following the programme.

Special schools are administered as primary schools and so the length of the school day in these schools is generally shorter than the school day in a mainstream post-primary school. While at a first glance it may seem that JCSP students in special schools have less instructional time than their counterparts in mainstream post-primary schools this may be alleviated somewhat by the fact that primary schools have a longer school year (183 days) than post-primary schools (167 days). It is recognised, however, that the shorter school day in special schools does make it more difficult to organise and implement the JCSP than is the case with mainstream post-primary schools. It is important, however, that the additional sixteen school days available in special schools would be used to remedy to the greatest extent possible the deficit in instructional time for students arising from the shorter school day.

While the JCSP may be suited to the needs of students with special educational needs, primarily because of its flexibility and its emphasis on the individual student, it was not specifically designed with such students in mind. The primary purpose of the JCSP (as described in some detail in sections 2.3 and 2.4) is to retain in the education system those students who are identified as being in danger of leaving school early, perhaps without completing the Junior Certificate. Notwithstanding this, one of the findings of this evaluation has been that many students with special educational needs might not have attained any formal qualification were it not for their participation in the JCSP, and might indeed have left school early. From schools' perspective the JCSP, with its curricular independence and cross-curricular and short-term targets, seems well suited to meeting the needs of students with special educational needs, while at the same time meeting the needs of its original target group. The issue, therefore, arises as to whether the JCSP should constitute the post-primary sector's main response to the needs of students with special educational needs. Can the JCSP meet the needs of two groups of students that, while sharing certain characteristics, have many differing needs, and where within each of the groups is a diverse range of abilities? To adequately meet the needs of both groups, the range of topics and profiling statements within the JCSP would need to be extended. Curricular issues and teaching and learning methodologies would also need to be addressed.

6.6 Summary of findings and recommendations

6.6.1 Findings

The following is a summary of the main findings in relation to the student selection procedures for the JCSP used by those schools that participated in the evaluation.

- Academic attainment, as reflected in students' assessment results on entry to post-primary school, is the principal criterion by which most schools select students for the JCSP.
- Not all schools involve primary schools and parents in student selection procedures.
- The JCSP, with its curricular independence and cross-curricular and short-term targets, seems well suited to meeting the needs of students with special educational needs, while at the same time meeting the needs of its original target group.
- The shorter school day in special schools makes it more difficult to implement the JCSP.

6.6.2 Recommendations

The following recommendations are made with regard to the selection of students for the JCSP by schools.

Recommendations for schools

- Schools should develop and foster an awareness of the benefits of the JCSP among parents and primary schools through such means as visits to primary schools, open days and information evenings.
- The selection of students for JCSP should include:
  - the involvement of senior management and the JCSP team
  - liaison between primary and post-primary schools at an early stage
  - the involvement of parents in the selection process
  - use by schools of a wide range of recognised indicators of risk of early school leaving
  - ensuring that any assessment tools used are appropriate, up-to-date, norm-referenced and culturally fair

- There should be follow-up by schools to the initial assessment carried out. This would ensure that all students who might benefit from the JCSP can continue to participate in the programme, while those who might no longer require the support of the JCSP can avail of the opportunity to follow the mainstream Junior Certificate programme.

Recommendations for policy-makers and policy advisers

- The JCSP Support Service, in conjunction with NEPS, should develop and disseminate appropriate guidelines to schools on best practice for the selection of students for the JCSP, including the assessment instruments to be used.
- Consideration should be given to how JCSP can best continue to meet the needs of post-primary students with special education needs. The Special Education Support Service (SESS) and the JCSP Support Service, in collaboration with other relevant stakeholders, should address this issue.

7   Staying With It
Participation and Retention

7.1   Introduction

This chapter examines issues pertaining to the participation and retention of students in the JCSP. The first part looks at home-school links and in particular the role of the HSCL co-ordinator. Attention is given here to the JCSP postcard system, which is one of the programme's main strategies in maintaining strong links between school and home. The next part of the chapter addresses the personal and pastoral supports made available to JCSP students, including the guidance support for students. The chapter concludes by looking at issues of student punctuality, attendance, and retention.

7.2   Home-school links

School inspection reports referred to the efforts made by schools to involve and inform parents, and to keep them informed, about the JCSP. The majority of reports commented that home-school links were very strong. Some schools were found to have been unsuccessful at involving parents in the programme in a meaningful way while others were innovative and resourceful in overcoming the reluctance of parents to engage with the programme. Some schools, for example, made it easier for parents to visit the school.

> The location of the main JCSP classrooms, close to an exit onto the street, facilitates regular short visits by parents when delivering and collecting their children. The fact that there is a parents' room provided in the same block affords easy and frequent access for brief, regular contact between parents and teachers.

Another inspection report commented on the provision of offices and small rooms in the school *"where meetings with parents can take place in comfort and privacy"*. All schools should foster such contact through easy access and a welcoming approach for parents.

7.2.1   Opportunities for contact between home and school

It was found that schools implement a wide range of strategies and activities aimed at developing home-school links for JCSP students. When surveyed, HSCL co-ordinators listed the following strategies as being frequently used:

- information evenings
- parent-teacher meetings
- coffee mornings or parents' afternoons
- celebration events
- home visits by members of the school staff
- letters and phone calls to parents
- JCSP brochures, postcards and newsletters
- the use of student journals for communication
- visits to the school by parents

Other examples of involving parents in the JCSP included inviting parents to the school to view samples of their children's work and to meet JCSP teachers, as well as sending students' work and projects home so that the students could show them to their parents.

It was found, however, that events that involve parents attending functions in the school provided the best opportunities for effective contact between home and school. The first opportunity for this type of contact occurred when students were being selected for participation in the JCSP. Although some schools communicated in writing with parents to explain the programme, others provided open days or information evenings for the parents of prospective students. This option, according to one inspection report, has certain long-term benefits:

> A dedicated meeting for parents of JCSP students, particularly parents of first year students, would provide a forum at which to explain the JCSP, and in which to outline the advantages for students in participating in the programme. Such contact could provide advance information and encouragement to parents and thus enlist their support for the effort of the school to assist students experiencing learning difficulties.

This approach provides schools with a good opportunity to obtain the views of parents, as well as any relevant background information on students. To build further on the home-school relationship fostered at this first meeting there could be follow-up meetings, perhaps early in the first year of the programme, that would keep parents briefed on the child's progress in their new programme and school. It was found, however, that only a small number of schools conducted such follow-up meetings.

Special JCSP events, such as the presentation of student profiles and Christmas celebrations, also provided occasions for parents to visit schools. However, the staging of such events requires a certain level of resources, and these were not always readily available in schools.

While one-third of the inspection reports referred to a high attendance of parents at JCSP events, in other schools involvement by parents proved problematic. Some reports referred to a "cultural bias against the institution of school" on the part of parents, while attendance at events by parents was reported to drop somewhat after their child's first year in school. In their questionnaire responses, two-thirds of the HSCL teachers stated that attendance by parents at JCSP events was either "very high" or "high," while one-third stated that it was "low" or "very low." Some of their comments regarding this area included:

> *"Parents from very disadvantaged backgrounds are more likely to attend celebrations/award presentations rather than information meetings"*
>
> *"It is more effective if home visits are made before JCSP events at which parents are expected to attend, this encourages participation"*
>
> *"Parent attendance levels are satisfactory – although many parents have the best intentions, life and trying issues at home get in the way"*

Home visits by school personnel, such as the HSCL co-ordinator, learning-support teacher or resource teacher for Travellers, foster home-school links. Occasionally, in schools in the SCP, co-ordinators of that programme visited the homes of JCSP students.

7.2.2 The role of the HSCL co-ordinator

Of the thirty schools that participated in the evaluation twenty-two had HSCL co-ordinators. While the responsibility for promoting home-school relations in the JCSP rests with the management of schools and JCSP teams in general, the majority of these HSCL co-ordinators had a special responsibility in this area. The HSCL co-ordinator generally played a role, for example, in the various activities and strategies employed by schools to develop links such as those listed in section 7.2.1.

In their questionnaire responses HSCL co-ordinators suggested the following as methods of developing the involvement by parents in the JCSP:

- involving parents in classroom activities, and as assistants to teachers
- more home visits by the HSCL teacher; the JCSP co-ordinator should also be involved, and parents of JCSP students themselves could help out in this respect
- developing interesting statements that parents and students could work on together
- clearer identification, through more home visits, of parents who never attend
- arranging "fun" nights – for example, parents and children going bowling
- the HSCL co-ordinator and JCSP co-ordinator possibly inviting reluctant parents, one to one, to view completed students' work
- encouraging parents to assist in clubs run by the school
- more seminars or talks for parents on topics in which they have an interest

7.2.3 JCSP postcards

A unique feature of the JCSP is the series of special postcards for use by teachers.

Figure 7.1 JCSP postcards

These postcards are designed to convey positive messages and are used by schools to help build the self-esteem of students, to help to predispose them positively towards school and to keep parents informed of their children's progress in school. The postcards were described in one inspection report as providing:

> an opportunity for a positive message about the students to come directly to the parents and thereby assist in breaking down the barriers that can exist between the school and the home.

In the main, inspection reports noted that the postcards were used effectively by schools to enhance home-school links, and to provide positive feedback on students' progress. It was reported in one school, for example, that the use of the postcards had a positive impact on the attendance of first-year students. It was also reported, however, that not all schools, or teachers, made use of the postcards. Some twenty per cent of inspectors' reports made recommendations encouraging the use of the postcards. Also, when interviewed students in only half of the schools stated that postcards were sent home. In those cases where the postcards were sent home, students reported that receiving them made their parents very happy.

Almost all of the twenty-two HSCL co-ordinators who completed evaluation questionnaires stated that the JCSP postcards were either "very effective" or "moderately effective." Some of their comments included:

> *"Parents love them, they regularly mention them to me"*
>
> *"I have visited homes where JCSP postcards and other positive reports take pride of place, I wish other teachers could see this"*
>
> *"Students are delighted to receive these cards, it makes them feel very important and valued"*

It is evident from inspectors' reports that sending a postcard home, which is a simple action, has a beneficial effect on JCSP students. It is unfortunate, therefore, that they are not used more frequently by some schools. It is recommended that schools and individual JCSP teachers should use the postcards to enhance positive contacts between school and the homes of students.

7.3 Pastoral care and personal support for JCSP students

An emphasis on pastoral care and the provision of a wide range of personal supports to meet the needs of students are vital components of the JCSP. Pastoral care strategies employed by schools to address students' needs, as described in inspection reports, included:

- individual meetings and group work with the guidance counsellor
- regular individual contact with the JCSP co-ordinator, class tutor, and other members of the staff
- homework clubs and "buddy programmes"
- primary to post-primary transfer programmes
- positive discipline programmes

Positive discipline programmes are aimed at encouraging the creation of a positive learning environment, minimising problems, and fostering respect and positive behaviour. Twenty-six of the JCSP co-ordinators surveyed indicated that their school implemented positive discipline programmes as a strategy to prevent early school leaving. The following quotation from an inspection report describes the operation of a positive discipline programmes in one school:

> The "discipline for learning" policy, which is in any case the whole school's approach to discipline and behaviour, helps to minimise problems and to encourage respect and positive behaviour among the students. Its aim is to create a positive learning environment, and this is largely achieved by its implementation. Problems are dealt with at class teacher, JCSP co-ordinator, deputy principal and principal level, and an air of respect prevails in the school. This greatly assists in the running of the JCSP, as the system is accepted by the whole school.

The approach to discipline outlined here is one that is conducive to a positive experience of the JCSP by all participants. It is recommended that in order to further enhance students' experience of JCSP that schools should adopt a positive discipline approach in their code of student behaviour.

The JCSP team, including the JCSP co-ordinator, the guidance counsellor, and the learning-support and resource teachers, were generally the personnel involved in organising pastoral care activities. In addition to activities that were provided during the school year, students were also supported during out-of-school times (e.g., some activities would be organised to take place during school holidays). The SCP, where it was available, played a significant role in this provision.

Carefully planned pastoral care strategies are necessary to provide students with a positive experience of school and they encourage the formation of a strong bond between schools and students. Schools should prioritise the development of these strategies, particularly in the case of JCSP students.

7.3.1 Guidance activities in the JCSP

The principal source of data on the provision of guidance in the JCSP was found in the responses by guidance counsellors to the questionnaires, to which nineteen counsellors responded. Table 7.1 outlines the extent of the involvement that these nineteen guidance counsellors had with JCSP students.

Activities	Proportion of guidance counsellors
Meeting third-year students	74%
Offering personal counselling to JCSP students	74%
Meeting the parents of JCSP students	68%
Liaison with other agencies on behalf of JCSP students	68%
Meeting first-year JCSP students	58%
Meeting second-year JCSP students	37%

Table 7.1 Guidance counsellors' engagement with JCSP students

While the proportion of guidance counsellors engaging in the different activities is relatively high, it must be borne in mind that guidance counsellors in eleven of the schools that participated in the evaluation did not respond. This may indicate that those particular guidance counsellors had little, or no involvement with JCSP students, and would therefore be a reflection of a low priority accorded to guidance for JCSP students in those schools.

Guidance counsellors also reported on the type of guidance service provided at each year level to JCSP students. The following were given as examples of activities organised for first-year students:
- individual meetings (often during the first week of post-primary schooling)
- individual meetings with students as needed
- administering assessment tests
- preparing students for transition to second year
- meeting students while they are still in primary school, and meeting parents
- personal development
- anti-bullying information

The following were given as examples of activities organised for third-year students:

- careers classes, including interviews, and employment options
- individual meetings with students as needed
- discussion on subject choice for senior cycle (e.g., LCA)
- study skills workshops
- attendance at weekly school meetings regarding special-needs students
- courses on personal skills or decision-making
- administering aptitude tests
- meeting parents

Guidance counsellors were often concerned with supporting students in making the transition from primary to post-primary school, while in third year they were generally concerned with supporting the transition to the senior cycle and providing information on out-of-school options. The provision of information on careers also featured at this level.

While guidance counsellors make a contribution to the JCSP in many schools, in others there was little involvement by them. In nearly one-third of the schools evaluated, for example, the inspectors recommended a role, or a greater role, for guidance in the JCSP, particularly in third year. It is recommended that guidelines on the provision of guidance or counselling within the JCSP should be developed for schools so that schools themselves can develop programmes for guidance in JCSP. The JCSP Support Service could contribute to their development.

7.3.2   Other staff members involved in providing support for students

A broad range of school personnel, other than guidance counsellors, was found to be involved in providing supports for JCSP students. In particular, the JCSP co-ordinator had a significant role in addressing the pastoral care needs of students in most schools. This was exemplified in one inspection report:

> The fact that the JCSP co-ordinator teaches the first year class twelve times a week helps to establish a solid rapport with the class group following the programme. Student difficulties are thus more easily spotted and dealt with at an early juncture.

Resource and learning-support teachers predominantly addressed students' learning difficulties in schools. In one school in particular the resource teacher for Travellers was ensuring the full integration of Traveller students in the school community, including the JCSP. School principals and class tutors were also involved in addressing difficulties experienced by students.

> The principal has given a great deal of time … to talking … with JCSP students who are experiencing difficulties. Frequently the student's parent/guardian is also present at this session with the principal. This non-confrontational format has been successful in continuing to motivate at-risk JCSP students to stay at school and to participate positively in the programme.

One school had a student welfare officer, funded through the SCP, while in another the VEC psychologist visited twice weekly to meet teachers and to assess students.

7.4   Punctuality, attendance, and retention

Inspection reports generally indicated that schools accorded considerable priority to student attendance. Issues of concern in this area include the frequency with which attendance is monitored by schools, whether there is appropriate follow-up where necessary, the extent of students' awareness that their attendance is being monitored, and the schools' own knowledge of the success of their efforts in this area. Inspection reports regarding twenty-five of the thirty schools evaluated referred to the systems that existed for monitoring attendance and punctuality, and almost all stated that the school had effective strategies for such monitoring. Some of these strategies involved schools:

- having either the principal, deputy principal, class tutor or SCP co-ordinator in charge of monitoring attendance
- having a specific teacher in charge of attendance
- calling the class register at regular intervals
- having a separate phone line for dealing with student absenteeism
- holding meetings between JCSP and SCP co-ordinators to monitor attendance

As an intervention to address the issue of early school leaving, the monitoring of attendance and punctuality is at the core of the JCSP. Inspectors regularly reported that students were aware that their attendance and punctuality were being closely monitored, but this was not the practice in all schools. In some schools attendance was checked during each lesson, while in others it was not as frequent. There was no evidence of attendance being monitored, for example, in thirty-one per cent of 115 lessons observed and rated with regard to attendance. In some instances absenteeism was a significant issue for schools. As a result, schools should give greater attention to the monitoring of attendance and punctuality. All JCSP teachers, for example, should keep records of attendance and punctuality for their classes. Further, where applicable, schools should devise a system of centrally collating this information, and communicating it to the home.

Sometimes the SCP helped fund follow-up procedures for monitoring the attendance and punctuality of JCSP students, which included in one instance the employment of a separate home-school resource person. Follow-up to absenteeism was predominantly carried out by phone calls, letters home, or home visits. One inspection report commented:

> Mechanisms through which the students themselves may become more conscious of their own levels of attendance and punctuality have been used to some extent, but are currently under review and a new arrangement is planned.

Various strategies to encourage attendance and punctuality were noted, such as rewards, writing positive comments in students' journals, or the use of JCSP stickers. Interestingly, it was found that JCSP postcards were not generally used to reward good attendance and punctuality. In some inspection reports there was a recommendation that schools explore other strategies for encouraging attendance and punctuality.

Opportunities to participate in out-of-school activities could be offered as an incentive for good attendance and participation in school.

The principal source of evidence available regarding whether the JCSP has resulted in an improvement in attendance by students, or in their retention at school, is the impression of the schools themselves. It is clear from the questionnaire responses of the HSCL and SCP co-ordinators that they feel that attendance and retention had improved as a result of the JCSP. Comments made by HSCL co-ordinators in this respect include:

"Because students enjoy tasks, they come to school more often and are less likely to drop out"

"Some students are staying on for LCA who might otherwise have left"

"Retention to senior level has improved since JCSP is meeting the needs of students"

"Very high attendance in general by JCSP students"

"Retention is good. Attendance varies"

"Attendance has improved because JCSP students feel a sense of ownership of their work"

"Retention rates are significantly higher, as we have a special class following JCSP"

Much of the evidence on improvements in student attendance and retention rates is anecdotal, as schools do not generally isolate and subject the relevant data to analysis. To assess the long-term success of the JCSP at improving attendance and retention, schools should keep records of students' progression after completion of the junior cycle. This information could be used by a school to inform its planning or self-evaluation process. It could also be aggregated nationally to measure more precisely the success of the JCSP at improving student attendance and retention. (This issue is given further consideration in chapter 10.)

7.5 Summary of findings and recommendations

7.5.1 Findings

The following is a summary of the main findings in relation to students' participation and retention in the JCSP for those schools that participated in this evaluation.

- Some schools have been resourceful and innovative in overcoming the reluctance of parents to engage with schools and with the JCSP, others have not been so successful.
- Although JCSP postcards can have a beneficial effect on JCSP students in building their self-esteem and helping to predispose them positively towards school, not all schools make use of them.
- While guidance and counselling play a significant role in the JCSP provided by many schools, in nearly one-third of the schools inspectors recommended a role, or a greater role, for guidance.
- Currently, much evidence on the improvements in students' attendance and retention is anecdotal.

7.5.2 Recommendations

The following recommendations are made with regard to improving procedures concerning students' participation and retention in the JCSP.

Recommendations for schools

- Schools should foster regular contact between home and school. Also, all teachers should use JCSP postcards in a systematic way.
- Schools should adopt a positive discipline approach in their code of student behaviour.
- Schools should develop and implement a pastoral care policy or strategy for JCSP students.
- Schools should provide JCSP students with guidance, including career advice, and counselling.
- Schools should implement effective systems for recording and monitoring attendance and punctuality in the JCSP.

Recommendations for policy-makers and policy advisers

- Guidelines on the provision of guidance and counselling within the JCSP should be developed for schools.
- School records of students' attendance and their destination after completing the junior cycle should be aggregated nationally in order to more accurately determine the success of the JCSP at improving attendance and retention.

8 What Happens in the JCSP?

The JCSP Curriculum

8.1 Introduction

This chapter is concerned with the curriculum of the JCSP in the schools evaluated. The issues involved in determining the curriculum for students, and the extent to which literacy, numeracy and the personal and social development of students are reflected in schools' curricula, are addressed. Learning support, which is an essential part of the JCSP, is also considered, as is the role of the JCSP in meeting the needs of students with special educational needs.

8.2 Breadth and range of the JCSP curriculum

While the breadth and range of the JCSP curriculum can vary from school to school each school must make at least two decisions regarding its JCSP curriculum:

- Each school must decide on the content of its JCSP curriculum
- Each school must decide on the teaching time to be allocated to each subject on the curriculum

8.2.1 Content of the JCSP curriculum

Table 8.1 gives the factors that, according to JCSP co-ordinators, influenced their schools' choice of JCSP curriculum.

How is the curriculum for the JCSP developed?	Proportion of co-ordinators or schools
Inclusion of students' project work	90%
Reduced number of examination subjects	86.7%
Based on results of assessment of students' abilities	86.7%
Development of students' numeracy skills	83.3%
Development of students' literacy skills	80%
Inclusion of cross-curricular work	76.7%
Developed in co-operation with members of the JCSP teaching team	70.0%

Table 8.1   Influences on the development of schools' JCSP curricula

It can be seen that for approximately twenty per cent of schools the development of literacy and numeracy skills is not a high priority. This trend is at odds with one of the fundamental aims of the JCSP whereby a school-wide approach to literacy and numeracy development should be part of the JCSP framework. Similarly, it can be seen from this table that a significant number of schools do not take students' abilities into account when constructing their JCSP curriculum, nor do many of them adopt a team approach to developing the curriculum. This finding points to the need for the managements of schools and their staffs to work together when developing the JCSP curriculum, and for them to consider the ability of their students' when devising the curriculum.

Table 8.1 also indicates that a significant proportion (i.e., 86.7%) of JCSP co-ordinators stated that reducing the number of examination subjects taken by students was one of the central principles in determining the JCSP curriculum in their school. However, inspectors found that this was not the case in a significant number of the thirty schools that participated in the evaluation. Data pertaining to the 2002 JCSP examinations were readily available for nineteen of these schools. From this data it was found that students took eleven examination subjects in the JCSP in two schools, four schools had students who took ten subjects in the examination while eleven schools had students who took nine subjects in the examination. The average number of examination subjects taken by students in the 2002 JCSP examination in the thirty schools evaluated was seven. While some JCSP students are undoubtedly capable of studying the full range of examination subjects at Junior Certificate level, a reduced number of subjects does allow for extra lessons in some subject areas, hence providing students with the opportunity to achieve at a higher level in these areas.

Table 8.2 shows the proportion of those thirty schools that participated in the evaluation in which each subject was taught in each of the three years of the programme. This table is based on the questionnaire responses of JCSP co-ordinators. As can be seen it was only in a small number of mainstream schools that students took a reduced number of subjects in the Junior Certificate examination. The number of subjects offered to JCSP students varied significantly from school to school, and these were not always dictated by the needs of the students. It was found that an average JCSP class in a post-primary school had in the region of twelve subjects on its curriculum. In seven schools, inspectors considered that the number of subjects studied was too great.

Subject	First year	Second year	Third year
English	100%	100%	100%
Mathematics	100%	100%	100%
Religion	92.3%	92%	92%
Art, craft, and design	88.5%	88%	88%
Physical education	88.5%	84%	88%
Home economics	80.8%	76%	76%
CSPE	65.4%	68%	68%
Computer studies (ICT)	61.5%	60%	52%
Irish cultural studies	57.7%	56%	40%
Geography	53.8%	48%	40%
SPHE	50%	48%	40%
Material technology (wood)	46.2%	56%	64%
History	42.3%	36%	36%
Irish	38.5%	40%	52%
Science	38.5%	48%	40%
Metalwork	30.8%	48%	52%
Social education	30.8%	28%	16%
Modern European language	26.9%	20%	16%
Technology or technical graphics	19.2%	20%	20%
Music	15.4%	32%	24%
Business studies	15.4%	12%	24%
Drama, dance, and choir	7.7%	12%	0
Reading	7.7%	8%	8%

Table 8.2   JCSP curriculum: proportion of schools with subject on the curriculum by year

English and Mathematics were included on the curriculum of all schools evaluated, while either Irish or Irish Cultural Studies was offered in almost all, as were religious education, physical education, and art, craft and design. Apart from this there was no clear pattern to the remainder of the subjects offered. Home Economics, CSPE and Computer Studies featured on the curriculum in each year of the programme in over fifty per cent of schools evaluated. Geography, SPHE and Materials Technology (Wood) were also well represented. Of the schools evaluated twenty-four per cent included Business Studies in the third year of their JCSP, while fewer than twenty per cent included a modern European language. One of the distinguishing characteristics, however, of the JCSP curriculum of many schools was the clear emphasis placed on practical subjects. The majority of schools in the evaluation included a number of practical subjects in their JCSP curriculum; in only two instances did inspectors comment that the subjects in the JCSP were either too academic or not practically focused.

It was found that Irish Cultural Studies replaced Irish on the curriculum in many schools. It was also found that the majority of JCSP students studying Irish Cultural Studies courses were not exempt from studying Junior Certificate Irish in accordance with Department of Education and Science Circular M10/94 – *Revision of Rule 46 of the "Rules and Programme for Secondary Schools" in relation to exemption from Irish*[10]. While there are certain merits in the Irish Cultural Studies courses being offered, these courses should supplement, and not replace, the study of Irish. For this reason, it is recommended that the relevant schools should review the place of Irish Cultural Studies in their JCSP curriculum and give appropriate consideration to including foundation level Junior Certificate Irish on their JCSP curriculum.

Data on the time allocated to the different subjects included in the JCSP curriculum in those schools that participated in the evaluation are included in Appendix 4. About half of the schools evaluated allocated approximately two hours (or three lesson periods) per week, or less, to Irish or Irish Cultural Studies. Most schools had allocated two hours per week or less for Science in second and third year. The emphasis on literacy and numeracy in the JCSP was reflected in some schools by the allocation of more than four hours each per week to Mathematics and English. In contrast, European languages fared poorly, with most students having fewer than two hours per week.

8.2.2 Timetabling the JCSP curriculum

Devoting the early part of the school day to the core or more academic type subjects (such as Mathematics and English), with practical and outdoor activities being scheduled in the afternoon, is considered good timetabling practice in the JCSP. In some of the schools evaluated it was found that students were not allocated the appropriate amount of instruction time in some of their subjects[11]. Inspectors reported, for example, that timetables for JCSP students in some schools were curtailed in the afternoons, with the result that these students had a short school day. This is not only poor timetabling practice but is also an infringement on a student's right to his/her education. Such short days were also found not to be in compliance with Department of

---

10   Department of Education and Science circular M10/94 – *Revision of Rule 46 of the "Rules and Programme for Secondary Schools" in relation to exemption from Irish* – details the circumstances under which students may be exempted from the study of Irish at junior cycle level. This circular can be found at www.education.ie.

11   NCCA guidelines state that 230 hours teaching or class contact hours are required to effectively cover any junior cycle syllabus.

Education and Science circular M29/95 – *Time in School*[12]. JCSP students are entitled to the same amount of instruction time as all other junior cycle students. It is essential that the restriction on instruction time for some JCSP students should be discontinued.

8.3   Subject areas in the JCSP curriculum

While Table 8.2 gives an insight into the range of subjects provided on the JCSP curriculum in schools, three subject areas in particular warrant comment. These are:

- languages
- practical subjects
- ICT

8.3.1   Languages

As mentioned in section 8.2.1, fewer than one-fifth of those schools evaluated were found to include a modern European language on their JCSP curriculum. This is reflected in State Examinations Commission data for the school year 2002/2003, which gives details of the numbers of JCSP students who took a modern European language in their Junior Certificate examination. This data is given in Table 8.3. The number of students who took English is included to give an indication of the size of the JCSP cohort.

Language	Number of JCSP students	Proportion of group
English	1,518	100%
French	216	14%
Italian	88	5.8%
Spanish	36	2.3%
German	23	1.5%

Table 8.3   Comparison of numbers of JCSP students taking languages, 2002/2003

The widespread practice of schools not offering students languages other than English and Irish is a matter of concern. It is clear that the majority of schools are of the view that the current syllabi pertaining to modern European languages at junior cycle are inappropriate or do not cater for the needs of JCSP students. It is recommended that the NCCA, in collaboration with the JCSP Support Service, should develop and support the implementation of suitable programmes in modern European languages for the JCSP.

8.3.2   Practical subjects

Practical subjects, such as Art, Craft and Design, Home Economics, and the technology-based subjects – e.g., Materials Technology (Wood) and Metalwork – feature prominently in the JCSP curriculum. During visits by the inspectors to practical subject lessons it was observed that students were virtually always actively engaged in precise operations, team work was evident, and appropriate safety procedures were being observed at all times. The benefits of these subjects for students was explained in one inspection report:

> PE, Art, Music and Drama in the curriculum provide an opportunity for
> confidence building and for the interaction of individuals with their peers.

---

12 Department of Education and Science circular M29/95 – *Time in School* – details the minimum number of teaching days per school year at 167 days, the minimum number of instruction hours per week at 28 hours, the minimum number of instruction hours per school day at 6 hours and the minimum number of instruction hours per half-day at 3 hours. This circular can be found at www.education.ie.

It was found that students derived a great sense of achievement and pride from engaging with design-and-make type exercises in their technology-based lessons, and they very often took project work home. This did much to advance home-school liaison. In summary, practical subjects in the JCSP curriculum meet a wide range of students' needs and aspirations and so tend to enhance the general quality of the programme. Access to these subjects by students should be encouraged.

8.3.3   ICT

ICT was sometimes used to enhance the teaching and learning process. Inspectors reported, for example, that ICT was used effectively as a teaching tool in forty per cent of those schools evaluated. ICT also featured in the JCSP as a discrete subject on students' timetables. The following extract from one inspection report highlights the benefits to be gained from such lessons:

> JCSP students' ICT skills are improved through the teaching of keyboard skills and digital camera usage. ICT is also used as a tool in the curriculum with students using educational software, researching using the Internet and using … [computer applications] to complete project work.

The emphasis here is clearly on the development of students' ICT skills, but this emphasis was not evident in all cases where ICT lessons featured on students' timetables. In some instances there was no definitive structure to the ICT lessons provided, and students were generally allowed to explore the technology in their own way.

Given the pervasiveness of ICT in practically every facet of modern life, it is disappointing that some schools did not expose students to ICT at all; and while others did so it was done in limited ways. Schools should exploit the possibilities presented by ICT in learning and teaching on the programme. Students could, for example, be provided with ICT lessons, and ICT could be integrated into many areas of the JCSP curriculum. The JCSP Support Service should develop guidelines for schools on how ICT could be effectively integrated into teaching and learning in the JCSP.

8.4   Orientation of the JCSP curriculum

The JCSP is characterised by an emphasis on developing students' literacy and numeracy skills and on enhancing their personal and social development. Cross-curricular activities, celebrations and out-of school activities are elements of the JCSP curriculum that specifically deal with students' personal and social development.

8.4.1   Literacy

The promotion of literacy skills is a core aim of the JCSP. In general, this happens at three levels in the programme:
- the development of literacy skills in lessons
- the development of a culture of reading
- other initiatives to promote literacy.

All these elements, however, should be underpinned by a whole-school policy and approach to literacy.

Development of literacy skills in lessons

In cases of best practice, literacy is a core element of all lessons in the JCSP. In twenty-five of the schools evaluated inspectors reported there being evidence of a strong emphasis on the development of literacy. In ten of these schools, for example, literacy development was central to the planning for the programme and was a unifying element in the cross-curricular work undertaken. Literacy was also promoted throughout the curriculum, with subject teachers making use of various strategies, including:

- use of the JCSP "key word" charts to identify subject-specific vocabulary
- providing key words on photocopied sheets or on the board
- project work
- pre-teaching of vocabulary
- use of teacher-generated hand-outs or simplified texts in booklet form

Subject teachers reported that these strategies made Junior Certificate teaching materials more comprehensible by students.

By contrast, in five of the schools evaluated inspectors reported that the development of literacy skills appeared to be confined to English lessons. In other lessons in these schools it was clear that the development of literacy skills was not a priority, and in some instances students appeared to have great difficulty in coping with the reading demands of the subjects. In extreme cases students were copying material from the blackboard without having any understanding of its meaning. Greater attention should be given to the different literacy needs of students in such schools. It is recommended that common strategies for the development of literacy should be devised and implemented throughout the JCSP curriculum. It is important that all teachers take responsibility for the development of literacy in their subject area. Indeed, schools could provide whole-school staff development in the area of literacy.

Development of a culture of reading

Some schools used established reading regimes to help develop a culture of reading among JCSP students. Many of these predated the JCSP and may have been introduced through the initiative of individual teachers. For example, in one school a classroom assistant helped with the teaching of reading, while in two other schools, literacy tutors had been appointed who worked closely with the learning-support teacher in operating a system of withdrawal for literacy tutoring.

Underpinning the development of literacy skills and the success of a school's literacy policy was the availability of suitable reading materials. In many schools the library was used frequently for the promotion of reading, and appropriate books were made available to students. Mobile "book boxes", that were brought from classroom to classroom, paid dividends here. Some schools timetabled library sessions for students to enhance the culture of reading, while others had libraries that were created specifically for JCSP students. It is clear that the school library plays a major role in the development of students' literacy skills.

The 'JCSP Demonstration Library Project' was initiated in 2001. The main aim of this project was to establish whether a good library, which caters for the needs of students with literacy difficulties, impacts positively on their learning. A small number of such libraries are operating nationally, and these are staffed by professional librarians.

Other initiatives for promoting literacy

Other initiatives used to promote the development of literacy in many schools included the paired-reading, Make-a-Book and Readalong initiatives. These are organised for the most part by the JCSP Support Service. Paired reading was reported to be particularly successful when it was well planned, when reading partners had received training and when the books were well chosen. Also, Make-a-Book projects were frequently put on public display in schools.

The views of learning-support teachers on factors that contribute to an improvement in students' literacy skills are given in Table 8.4.

Factor	Proportion of learning-support teachers
Learning support	91%
Availability of statements and clearly defined goals for reading	86%
Small classes	86%
Extra resources	77%
Make-a-book	73%
Paired reading	64%
Readalong	46%
Small team of teachers	59%
Offering fewer subjects	68%

Table 8.4   Factors that contribute to improvement in literacy skills

It is noteworthy that none of the schools evaluated had a whole school literacy strategy, or a written literacy policy, and inspectors made recommendations in this regard. Each school providing the JCSP should develop a whole-school literacy strategy and use it to encourage subject teachers to give priority to literacy skills, leading to a culture of reading and of library use among students.

8.4.2   Numeracy

The development of students' numeracy skills – the ability to use appropriate mathematical knowledge, skills and experience in everyday life – is another principal aim of the JCSP. Unlike the development of literacy skills, which prevailed in a number of other subject areas besides English, in most of the schools evaluated the promotion of numeracy was considered to be principally, or in some cases solely, the remit of teachers of Mathematics or technology-based subjects. While there was no whole school numeracy strategy or policy in place in any of the schools visited, many examples of good practice in the development of numeracy skills were observed. Some of these included:

- 'Maths for Fun' lessons
- the use of computers, computer programs and calculators
- involving students in measuring
- working out calculations in project work
- the use of specially designed work sheets
- variety in the teaching of basic mathematical operations.

In one instance a range of kits or games designed to facilitate an understanding of different mathematical concepts were being used. Here the students worked at their own pace, and the teaching style accommodated their different capabilities and attainments. Similar practices were observed in the case of science and some technology-based subjects.

Learning support in numeracy was provided in some schools, although numeracy skills almost invariably received less attention in this respect than literacy skills. In a small number of schools each JCSP student had an individual numeracy development programme, with numeracy being continuously assessed. Few inspection reports referred to use being made of diagnostic testing in the area of numeracy.

The position and status of numeracy in the JCSP curriculum should be kept under continuous review by schools. A cross-curricular approach is appropriate with regard to numeracy and like literacy, all schools should develop a whole-school numeracy strategy. Schools should endeavour to emphasise the development of mathematical themes and concepts in all subject areas where such opportunities arise.

8.4.3   Social and personal development

The social and personal development of students is addressed in the JCSP in a variety of ways. There is formal provision in the timetable for promoting social and personal development through Social, Personal and Health Education (SPHE) lessons, pastoral care, or social education. Many schools place an emphasis on the personal and social development of students in the teaching of other subjects, in their expectation of good manners and politeness and in their concern for the promotion of students' self-esteem. Also, cross-curricular profiling statements on personal and social development are available and the JCSP teaching team will, in most cases, be involved in choosing and awarding these statements. Finally, social and personal development is also nurtured through various dedicated JCSP events or celebrations and involvement in extra-curricular activities.

Cross-curricular activities

The cross-curricular element of the JCSP involves engaging students in complementary activities in different subject areas, thus linking different parts of the curriculum. It was found that most of the schools that participated in the evaluation placed a strong emphasis on cross-curricular activities, and these were supported with student profiling statements. One inspection report drew attention to the rationale for cross-curricular work:

> Cross-curricular activities develop students' social skills, encourage co-operation, unify the learning experience of students and are an important focus of the JCSP.

Examples of cross-curricular activities included the organisation of musicals or concerts, horticultural schemes in which products were grown to be sold by a mini-company, and Christmas celebrations during which individual students read poems and prose that they had composed.

Celebrations

Almost all schools that participated in the evaluation held special celebration events for JCSP students during the school year. The most popular celebrations were those held at Christmas and at the awarding of student profiles towards the end of third year. Celebration events provide opportunities for increased motivation and also help to promote the JCSP programme and its curriculum, as well as the achievements of students.

In some schools, concerts or nativity plays were staged at celebration events and this enhanced the social and personal development potential of the occasion. This is captured in the following extract from one inspection report:

> The Christmas celebration entailed a nativity play, reading and speaking in public, and singing. Three individual students read poems and prose they had themselves composed. This was followed by a reception for their parents and families, which was attended by their teachers and management. The class had baked, prepared sandwiches and prepared the tables. They very competently served food and drinks and tidied up afterwards. It was an impressive demonstration of cross-curricular learning.

In another report:

> A mini-company has been set up – a wood technology and business studies joint venture, supported by Mathematics and English – to market wooden objects produced in the Materials Technology (Wood) lessons, to be sold at the Christmas celebration. These subjects/activities contribute to motivating both the individual and the group, enriching their experience of school life and extending their learning beyond the constraints of examination-oriented, subject-based learning.

Students are usually happy to welcome their parents to celebrations where awards and achievements are publicly recognised. However, as described in chapter 3, some schools reported difficulty in achieving good attendance by parents at certain events. Further restriction on the holding of celebration events was the lack of funds available. While some schools succeeded in raising funds for their events, others had to abandon them.

Out-of-school activities

JCSP students benefited from many out-of-school activities that contributed significantly to their personal development. Examples of these activities, as reported by JCSP co-ordinators, are given in Table 8.5. Many, it should be stated, are organised by the JCSP Support Service.

Initiative	Frequency
Readalong	96.2%
Celebrations	93.1%
Make-a-book	89.3%
Outdoor education	82.1%
Paired reading	75.9%
Competitions	70.0%
Music education	57.7%
Team-building	52.0%
JCSP student newsletter	44.4%

Table 8.5   JCSP activities in schools

Examples of outdoor educational activities included hill-walking, pitch and putt, swimming, visits to exhibitions and other centres, pool, indoor soccer, bowling, hurling, and go-karting. In some schools, however, teachers were reluctant to organise these types of activities. This may be attributed to teachers' fears of student indiscipline or public misbehaviour and the general risk associated with bringing students on trips. There was often the added problem of cost, though not all out-of-school activities proved expensive. Schools that participated in the SCP and other such initiatives often organised clubs or other activities to promote personal and social development, and students clearly benefited from these activities. It is recommended that schools should endeavour to provide JCSP students with a range of out-of-school activities in accordance with their needs and interests.

A school's code of behaviour has an effect on the personal and social development of students, and many of the schools visited (as reported in chapter 7) had positive discipline systems in place based on mutual respect, positive affirmation and transparency. During interviews held as part of this evaluation, JCSP students displayed a sense of maturity, they were courteous, confident and forthcoming, and it was evident that their self-esteem had benefited from their participation in the JCSP.

It is clear that the JCSP is successful at enhancing students' personal and social development. This should continue to be an emphasis of the programme.

8.5 Learning support

The provision of learning support is an important component of the JCSP, and in some schools the learning-support or resource teacher is also the JCSP co-ordinator. Many students participating in the programme have special educational needs, and in some schools all students that take the JCSP require learning support.

The identification of those students requiring learning support was generally based on the results of screening assessments and on the student's reading achievement level. Learning support in the schools evaluated was generally provided in literacy and numeracy. Other areas in which support was provided included helping students with other subjects on the curriculum, supporting them in the preparation of projects for the Junior Certificate examination, and nurturing their personal and social development.

Learning support was predominantly organised by means of a withdrawal system in schools. Other methods used, though to a lesser extent, included in-class support, team teaching, and teacher support. When surveyed, fifty-five per cent of learning-support teachers reported that all JCSP students in their school were receiving learning support. A similar proportion reported that parents were involved in the learning-support programme in their school. This involvement, however, ranged from a general awareness among parents of the JCSP and its associated learning supports and attendance at celebration events to a more active involvement, such as engaging in activities associated with reading challenges and paired reading.

A small number of schools had developed individual education programmes for students in need of learning support. These were generally designed to address the development of strengths and the remediation of particular learning difficulties.

8.6 Students with special educational needs

As stated in chapter 6, the JCSP is widely used by post-primary schools and special schools to cater for the needs of students with special educational needs. This section reviews those issues arising for the JCSP in catering for the curricular needs of these students.

It was found that many schools adapted the JCSP curriculum and their teaching methodologies to cater for the curricular needs of students with special educational needs. The principal sources of information in this regard were the questionnaires completed by JCSP co-ordinators and resource and subject teachers. Table 8.6 outlines some of the ways, according to each of the JCSP co-ordinators in the thirty schools that participated in the evaluation, in which schools have adapted the JCSP to accommodate students with special educational needs.

Adaptation	Proportion of co-ordinators	Example of response
Modified teaching methods	51.7%	Variety of teaching methods, multi-sensory learning
Modified syllabus	41.4%	JCSP tailored to meet these students needs at profiling meetings
Development of appropriate statements	20.7%	Some students have different statements, depending on ability
Smaller class or group size	20.7%	Smaller groups allow for positive interaction and learning
Fewer subjects	20.7%	Reduction in number of subjects
Withdrawal or resource teaching support	20.7%	Occasional withdrawal of students for one-to-one teaching
Team teaching or team approach	17.2%	Resource teachers liaise with practical teachers for projects or texts
Adaptation of instructional materials	13.8%	Relevant teachers are informed, and they seek suitable texts
Emphasis on success	10.3%	Students' strengths are built upon by choice of subjects, especially practical subjects
More instructional time	10.3%	Extra English and Mathematics lessons

Table 8.6 Adapting the JCSP to meet the needs of students with special educational needs

At the classroom level, subject teachers also adapted their programmes to cater for students with special educational needs. When surveyed, ninety-one per cent of subject teachers surveyed stated that they had students with special educational needs in their JCSP classes. Table 8.7 shows the principal adaptations made by these subject teachers to accommodate these students.

Adaptation of the JCSP to accommodate students with special needs	Proportion of teachers
Relevant or simplified materials	21.4%
Development of appropriate targets or statements	17.5%
Modified content or programme	13.0%
Appropriate task analysis	8.4%
More individual attention	6.5%

Table 8.7 Adaptations made by JCSP subject teachers to accommodate students with special educational needs

Teachers often obtained more relevant or simplified teaching materials outside the normal range of textbooks, using appropriate computer programs or preparing specialised worksheets.

For resource teachers, issues of modification of the curriculum involved students working towards statements based on their assessed needs, reducing the curriculum, emphasising the teaching of social skills or providing one-to-one teaching. It was the view of seventy-five per cent of those resource teachers surveyed that the JCSP was relevant and suitable for students with special educational needs. Their comments included:

> "Statements comprise easily manageable goals that provide students with an immediate sense of achievement"
>
> "The JCSP provides a strong support system to students"
>
> "Both teachers and students can monitor the achievement of targets"
>
> "Learning experiences are more relevant to students' aptitudes"
>
> "The JCSP leads to positive group and individual identities"
>
> "Gives recognition to aspects of learning that are valued"
>
> "Literacy and numeracy are enhanced"
>
> "Without JCSP, these students would have left school with no qualifications"
>
> "Statements make the junior cycle curriculum more accessible to students with special needs"

Resource teachers also suggested that the JCSP could be made even more relevant and suitable for students with special educational needs. The principal modifications suggested by these teachers included:

- The programme or statements need to be broadened to better address the needs of students with moderate or severe learning difficulties.
- More basic statements should be developed for all subjects.
- There should be more "student-friendly" language in JCSP statements.
- A less cumbersome approach to profiling should be developed.
- There should be a modification of CSPE statements to address students' needs.
- There should be more cross-curricular links.
- There is a need to constantly update materials.
- There should be more involvement by students in the choice of statements.
- There should be additional tasks for developing social skills, or stronger emphasis on social skills.
- The programme would benefit from exchanging ideas with teachers involved in the JCSP in other schools.

As already recommended in Chapter 6, for the JCSP to effectively meet the needs of students with special educational needs further development work would need to take place. In particular, curricular issues, including extending the range of topics and profiling statements within the JCSP, would need to be addressed, as would teaching and learning methodology issues. Further, the issues implicit in the comments of resource teachers above would need to be addressed.

The Special Education Support Service (SESS), in collaboration with the JCSP Support Service, should address the benefits of developing the JCSP to meet more directly the needs of students with special educational needs. Both services should also encourage schools that have students with special education needs and special schools providing the JCSP, to share insights, ideas and methods on how best to meet the needs of their students. Teachers would benefit from such networking opportunities.

8.7 Summary of findings and recommendations

8.7.1 Findings

The following is a summary of the main findings in relation to the JCSP curriculum of those schools that participated in this evaluation.

- Schools do not always consider students' abilities, or have a team approach, when developing their JCSP curriculum.
- It was found that JCSP students did not take a reduced number of Junior Certificate examination subjects in a significant number of the thirty schools that participated in the evaluation.
- It was found that well over half of the schools that participated in the evaluation did not provide students with Science, Irish or modern European languages as part of their curriculum. With regard to languages, for example, the proportion was as high as eighty per cent. In general, schools felt that the curriculum associated with these subjects was not appropriate for JCSP students.
- It was found that practical subjects meet a wide range of students' needs and aspirations and so tend to enhance the general quality of the programme for students.
- There is a great variety of practice with regard to the use of ICT in the JCSP. However, in a significant number of schools JCSP students do not engage with ICT.
- At the time of the evaluation no school had a written whole-school literacy or numeracy policy in place. In general it was found that the development of students' literacy and numeracy skills was considered to be within the remit of English and Mathematics or technology-based lessons only.
- The JCSP is successful at enhancing students' personal and social development. It was evident that students' self-esteem had benefited from participation in the JCSP.
- Most schools placed a strong emphasis on cross-curricular activity, including the organisation of musicals or concerts, mini-company work and Christmas celebrations.
- Withdrawing students from certain lessons was the principal method for organising learning support in almost all schools.

8.7.2 Recommendations

The following recommendations are made with regard to striving to improve the quality, effectiveness and relevance of schools' curriculum for JCSP.

Recommendations for schools

- School management and staff should work closely together when developing their JCSP curriculum. Also, the curriculum should be tailored to meet the needs and abilities of students.
- Schools should exploit the possibilities presented by ICT in both the administration of the programme and in learning and teaching.
- Irish Cultural Studies courses should supplement, and not replace, the study of Irish in the JCSP. Where relevant, schools should review the place of Irish Cultural Studies in their JCSP curriculum and give consideration to including foundation level Junior Certificate Irish.
- It is essential that the practice by some schools of shortening the school day for JCSP students be discontinued.
- Each school providing the JCSP should develop a whole-school literacy strategy. Attention should be given to the differing literacy needs of students in the teaching of the curriculum. All teachers should take responsibility for the development of literacy in their subject areas and schools should undertake whole-school staff development in this area.

- Each school providing the JCSP should develop a whole-school numeracy strategy. There should be a whole-school approach to numeracy throughout the programme, and this should be kept under continuous review. Diagnostic testing, which is used to determine students' numeracy levels, their needs, and their progress in numeracy development, should be used more frequently by schools.
- The development of students' social and personal skills should continue to be an emphasis of the JCSP.

Recommendations for policy-makers and policy advisers

- It has been recommended earlier in this report that consideration should be given to how the JCSP can best continue to meet the needs of post-primary students with special educational needs. Areas that warrant consideration here include:
  - personnel from mainstream schools that provide the JCSP as well as personnel from those schools that have students with special educational needs, and personnel from special schools that provide the JCSP, should come together to share insights, ideas, and methods
  - a greater range of student profiling statements throughout all subjects should be developed; also the language used in profiling statements should be clear and easily understood.
- The NCCA, in collaboration with the JCSP Support Service, should develop and support the implementation of suitable programmes in modern European languages for the JCSP.
- The JCSP Support Service should investigate how the use of ICT in the JCSP could be substantially developed in order to support teaching and learning.

9 Inside and Beyond the JCSP Classroom
Teaching and Learning

9.1 Introduction

Effective teaching and learning calls for planning of teaching activities, the use of a variety of teaching methods and involving students as much as possible in lessons. At the same time the needs of the individual student should be catered for, while all students need to be regularly affirmed for their efforts. In the JCSP effective teaching and learning also includes the use of profiling statements and learning targets.

This chapter examines the planning and preparation issues associated with the JCSP lessons observed in the schools evaluated, including planning for the use of profiling statements, learning targets and resources. The teaching methodologies employed in the JCSP lessons visited are also examined. Reference is made to the extent of students' participation in lessons and the nature of the learning atmosphere. Finally, this chapter examines the role and nature of student assessment in the JCSP, and mentions some of the ways in which student achievement is recognised.

The material in this chapter is based primarily on inspection reports, the lesson observation schedules that were completed by inspectors and the responses of JCSP personnel to questionnaires administered as part of the evaluation.

9.2 Lesson Planning and Preparation

It is important when preparing for teaching and learning in the JCSP that lessons are tailored to suit the student cohort concerned, with suitable resources being made available to support learning. The student profiling statements, and their associated learning targets, can be used to aid the planning process. They can help to focus planning and, in so doing, can contribute towards ensuring that the needs of individual students are catered for.

9.2.1 Planning for teaching and learning

Effective planning and preparation characterised lessons that were pitched at an appropriate level for students and that set clear tasks for them to complete. Such lessons had a clear focus, the teachers' presentation emphasised basic but important information, and the students were constantly affirmed for their efforts. These lessons were also well structured and had a clear progression from previously learned material.

Observation of teaching and learning indicated that teachers who carefully planned lessons and employed appropriate resources were successful in engaging the attention of students, and in making learning an enjoyable experience for them. Planning for lessons, including the use of resources, was reported as being "optimal" or "very good" in more than eighty per cent of the JCSP lessons observed by inspectors, while the appropriateness of teaching materials used was considered to be "optimal" or "very good" in more than ninety per cent of lessons observed. Planning for the use of resources frequently involved teachers in adapting teaching materials to make them more suitable for use with JCSP students. Many inspection reports, for example, included positive comments regarding the commitment shown by teachers in preparing specialised worksheets, hand-outs, or booklets. It was also found that some schools had spent considerable funds and effort on appropriate packages, or kits, to facilitate learning by students.

Some teachers reported that the lack of suitable teaching materials was a serious hindrance to effective teaching in the JCSP. In situations where the teaching materials were not considered appropriate for lessons it was usually because textbooks were too difficult for students, or hand-outs contained complex language. Also, in these lessons opportunities were generally not availed of to promote literacy skills. In some schools most of the funds and resources were concentrated in first year, which curtailed the quality of the teaching materials made available to students in the second and third years of the programme.

Schools should ensure that textbooks are appropriate to their students' needs, interests, and ability levels.

9.2.2   Profiling statements and learning targets

The use of profiling statements and learning targets in the JCSP, as detailed earlier in this report, lies at the core of the JCSP. It is through the use of learning targets that subjects are broken down into easily managed units of work, students become more aware of their progress, success is experienced more frequently, teachers collaborate on cross-curricular teaching and learning and each student can have an individual programme for learning.

While evidence was found of good practice in relation to the implementation of student profiling in most schools, this was not always the case. It was found, for example, that some schools often did not use statements and targets at all, their use was not always co-ordinated within a school, teachers did not always use them in a consistent manner and there were frequent administrative issues with regard to their use. Also, in many schools there was an emphasis on examination-focused teaching and learning, particularly with regard to third year students following the programme.

Effective planning requires careful selection of profiling statements and learning targets, and this needs to be backed up with a consistent approach to their use. In those lessons observed where there was a clear focus on learning targets it was obvious that teachers had previously discussed with their students what they aimed to do in their subject, and that this had informed the selection of easily attainable targets. Carefully selected targets, if this is done in collaboration with the student, help to give students a sense of achievement. The use of statements and targets in these lessons was fundamental to the teaching methods employed and to the progress made. This is illustrated in the following extract from one inspection report:

> Profiling statements are used … as the basic organisational tool through which various aspects of the prescribed curriculum for Junior Certificate subjects are made accessible and meaningful for the students.

While there was evidence of the use of statements and learning targets in many schools, there was less evidence regarding the existence of a co-ordinated approach to their use. In some cases statements were generally issued to all teachers by the programme co-ordinator, and then the teachers decided individually what learning targets would be worked on. Variation was also found in the manner in which teachers used profiling statements and learning targets. Sometimes students were responsible for the folders used for tracking their progress, with the help of their teachers. In other cases the JCSP co-ordinator or individual teachers kept the student's folders. This latter system, however, was somewhat flawed in that it tended to exclude the student's involvement in monitoring their individual progress towards specific targets. Evidence of students' progress, including the achievement of learning targets, should be accessible to students, teachers, and parents.

When students are aware of their statements and learning targets they will also be aware of the work that must be completed in order to reach the targets set. In schools where this was the case (i.e., where students were familiar with the profiling system) they were aware of the criteria for meeting each learning target. In the main their work was stored in a well-organised fashion in individual folders, which they used every day. They had "ownership" of the profiling statements and, where they filled them in regularly, could demonstrate their achievements. Students in these schools were reported to be enthusiastic about the programme. Regular feedback to students through the profiling system, according to questionnaire responses from JCSP co-ordinators, took place in just forty-three per cent of the schools.

While JCSP students in the majority of schools were in separate classes for almost all subjects, in other schools (as referred to in chapter 5) they studied some subjects in classes with non-JCSP students. These schools generally experienced difficulty in implementing the student profiling system, as the profiling applied to some students in a particular class group, but not to others in the same group. It is recommended that methods should be developed for monitoring students' progress in such circumstances, perhaps through an adaptation of the profiling system.

In some schools where student profiling was being implemented there were instances of folders not being regularly updated, as well as some that contained statements with missing details. A small number of inspection reports indicated that profiling statements and learning targets were not being used at all by teachers. Given the central importance of profiling to the JCSP, it is arguable as to whether such schools were actually implementing the JCSP at all. In a school where learning targets were not in use the inspection report commented that the students could not:

> identify any level of immediate progress and they received no acknowledgement of, or feedback on, their achievements.

Some teachers in schools that had not implemented the profiling system may have viewed it as excess paperwork and photocopying. Indeed, the burden of the paperwork generated by the profiling system was often referred to in inspection reports. This is an area with which JCSP co-ordinators and their teams had difficulties.

For many teachers, although they agreed with the underlying philosophy of the programme and profiling system, completing profiling statements was seen as a cumbersome system. This was particularly so in schools where large numbers of students were taking the JCSP.

It has already been suggested (see chapter 4) that the student profiling system be subjected to a thorough review with a view to exploring ways of reducing the administrative requirement of the system on schools. It has also been suggested that this review should explore the feasibility for a greater role for ICT in the administration of the profiling system. At school level, priority should be given to developing a streamlined approach to the recording and storing of profiling statements. Indeed the student profiling system should be organised, planned and co-ordinated in order to ensure that there is a consistent and coherent approach to the whole process. The JCSP teaching team should be collectively involved in selecting achievable learning targets for students.

The profiling system should be used with all students in the JCSP. This can significantly enhance the teaching and learning process and provide opportunities for positive feedback to students.

9.3 Inside the JCSP classroom

It is good practice in the JCSP classroom that certain aspects in teaching and learning are emphasised. The first of these, for example, is the need to develop students' literacy and numeracy skills. The second is the development of personal and social skills. Thirdly, in many JCSP classes there are students with special educational needs; this presents challenges for teaching and learning.

9.3.1 Literacy and numeracy in JCSP lessons

In their questionnaire responses, JCSP co-ordinators and teachers stated that they placed an emphasis on the development of literacy and numeracy skills in JCSP lessons. Just over forty-six per cent of subject teachers, for example, stated that they placed "a lot" of emphasis on developing students' literacy, while thirty-eight per cent indicated placing "some" emphasis on this skill. Numeracy featured to a lesser extent than literacy, with thirty-one per cent stating that they emphasised it "a lot" and thirty-two per cent stating that they placed "some" emphasis on it. However, these figures were not reflected in the 108 lessons observed and rated for attention to literacy and numeracy.

Attention to literacy and numeracy rated poorly, with forty-five per cent of lessons visited either having "scope for development" or "requiring major improvement" in the area. Inspectors made comments such as "keywords were not explained", "nothing was written on the chalkboard to assist literacy" and "students had no sense of identification with or were not provided with an interpretation of the text for reading". Lessons that paid "optimal" or "very good" attention to literacy and numeracy skills were described as having "keywords on the wall that teachers referred to regularly" or "reading materials were chosen and developed to assist students". In mathematics lessons, for example, it was stated that basic operations were "done fully on the blackboard". In general, there was a greater emphasis in the lessons observed on improving students' literacy than on numeracy skills.

In schools where it is not already the case greater attention needs to be given to the development of students' literacy and numeracy skills in JCSP lessons. The development of these skills should permeate all areas of the curriculum.

9.3.2 Personal and social development in JCSP lessons

When surveyed, just over sixty-four per cent of subject teachers reported that they placed a strong emphasis on personal and social development in JCSP lessons. In seventy lessons observed, ratings were assigned to attention paid to social and personal statements. In twenty-one per cent of these lessons the attention was rated as "optimal." Here, independent work was encouraged among students, they displayed a positive self-image, and the importance of showing respect for others was emphasised. Affirmation of students was reinforced by praise from the teacher, speaking to students individually, issuing rewards for good work or effort (such as stickers and stars), issuing JCSP postcards and regular reports to parents, and reviewing work against targets and statements. Many students were also affirmed for their learning achievements, for their contribution to and participation in lessons, and for their behaviour.

Attention to students' personal and social development was less evident in lessons that concentrated on subject-centred learning. This was the case for twenty-nine per cent of the seventy lessons rated for attention to the development of personal and social skills. It is important that the development of students' personal and social skills feature in all JCSP lessons, with use being made of appropriate profiling statements.

9.3.3   Students with special educational needs

Ninety-five per cent of teachers of JCSP classes in the schools that participated in this evaluation reported having students with special educational needs in their class groups. Students with special educational needs were catered for principally through the use of special needs assistants (SNAs), team teaching, withdrawal and special or resource classes. In most schools the resource and learning-support teachers tended to use the teaching approaches of the JCSP to a greater extent than other teachers.

Table 9.1 shows adaptations made by teachers to their teaching methods to accommodate students with special educational needs.

Adaptations made to teaching methods to accommodate students with special educational needs in classes	Proportion of teachers
More individual attention	18.8%
Practical activities	11.0%
Repetition or review	11.0%
Simplified or modified worksheets	11.0%
Visual presentation	10.4%
Slower pace	7.8%
Appropriate materials or texts	6.5%
Assessment to support learning	6.5%
Group work	6.5%
More demonstrations	5.8%
Use of ICT	5.2%
Task analysis or setting achievable targets	5.2%
Clear instructions	4.5%
Developmentally appropriate tasks	4.5%
SNA	4.5%
Modified, simplified language	3.9%

Table 9.1   Adaptations made to teaching methods to accommodate students with special educational needs

In cases where students are withdrawn from their base class for extra support, it is important that collaboration takes place between the resource or learning-support teachers and the subject teachers to ensure that the students learning needs are met. Ideally, for students with special educational needs collaborative planning should take place between the subject teachers and the resource or learning-support teachers, and this should concentrate on the expected outcomes of the Junior Certificate syllabus for the particular subject area.

9.4   Teaching and learning in the JCSP

Teaching and learning in the JCSP places demands on the teacher above and beyond those associated with mainstream classes. Special attention, for example, must be given to the teaching methodologies employed in lessons and to ensuring that students engage with or participate in lessons. The same level of attention must also be given to the nature of the classroom atmosphere and to the teacher's expectations of students.

9.4.1   Teaching methodologies

Inspectors reported on the extent to which teaching methodologies were varied and appropriate in 115 of the JCSP lessons observed. An "optimal" rating was given to thirty-five per cent of these lessons. In such lessons a wide range of methods was employed. These methods included group work, pair work, individual work and project work, computer-assisted learning, storytelling, use of the chalkboard or overhead projector, practical demonstrations, role-playing, cross-curricular work, discussion, hand-outs or worksheets, questioning and learning games and challenges. Teacher demonstrations were kept short; students often had prepared materials to work with, and the types of task set facilitated their success. The pace of teaching was varied in most of these lessons, and time was allowed for all students to progress at their own pace. There was regular reinforcement of learning, and this gave students confidence in what they had covered in the lessons. Most importantly, teacher inputs were at an appropriate level for each student. By implementing such methods teachers generally succeeded in adapting work to the needs and abilities of students.

Project work and group and pair work were generally commented upon favourably by inspectors. Group work in JCSP lessons was used predominantly to discuss issues and to prepare materials. There was evidence of detailed planning for project work, with clear and simple tasks being assigned to individual students, and much of the work observed was of a cross-curricular nature. One report, for example, described a project where Christmas trees with lights were made, with the co-operation of the Materials Technology (Wood) and art teachers.

In response to their questionnaire, eighty-eight per cent of the 145 subject teachers that responded stated that they had adapted their teaching methods for JCSP classes. Table 9.2 shows the most frequent adaptations that teachers made.

Examples of adaptations to teaching methods	Proportion of teachers
Appropriate teaching materials	17.2%
Practical activities	17.2%
Individual attention	16.6%
Slower pace, or student works at own rate	15.2%
Use of statements and learning targets	11.0%
Help with reading, literacy, vocabulary or spelling	9.7%

Table 9.2   Proportion of subject teachers reporting adaptations to teaching methods implemented in JCSP lessons

Teaching materials (as referred to in Table 9.2) included, for example, worksheets, material for overhead projectors and literacy materials adapted from a scheme for teaching literacy to adults. The provision of such material clearly involved extra preparation on the part of teachers. Practical activities included placing greater emphasis on the practical elements of Junior Certificate courses, particularly in Art, Craft and Design and in Science. Much of the attention given to students was individual instruction, based on particular learning targets for the student concerned. Several of the teachers who provided help with literacy referred to the keyword method of vocabulary development.

It is interesting to note that in response to their questionnaire sixty per cent of the 145 subject teachers that responded stated that participation in the JCSP had made a difference to the teaching methods they employed with non-JCSP students. The most frequent adaptations are shown in Table 9.3.

Examples of difference in teaching method	Proportion of teachers
Greater awareness of weaker students	30.8%
Broader range of teaching methods	11.0%
Modifying pace of teaching	7.7%
Paired work or group work	7.7%
Planning for or addressing individual needs	6.6%
Cross-curricular activities	5.5%
Target-setting (including students' involvement)	5.5%
More active teaching methods	4.4%

Table 9.3   Proportion of teachers reporting differences in teaching methods with non-JCSP classes

Only ten per cent of the 115 JCSP lessons observed and rated with regard to teaching methods were described as being "in need of major improvement". In such instances there was generally overuse of particular worksheets or over-reliance on the textbook. In these lessons the students were usually described as being passive or disengaged. There was usually an inappropriate balance between the inputs of the teacher and the inputs of the students, with the teacher dominating the lesson. This scenario was often accompanied by an emphasis on examinations, which often served to reduce the personal and social dimension of the programme.

Attention needs to be given to further tailoring teaching approaches and methods to the needs and interests of JCSP students. Teachers should be supported in this task by a whole-school emphasis on quality in teaching and learning. The JCSP Support Service also has an important role to play here.

9.4.2   Students' participation in lessons

Student participation in the lessons observed was heavily influenced by the attention given to individual students by teachers, and by the degree of involvement of each student in their own learning. A high level of attention was given to individual students in more than eighty per cent of the lessons visited. On the whole, personalised intervention was pitched at a level appropriate to the attainment and ability levels of students.

Students were considered to be actively involved in their learning in seventy-eight per cent of those lessons observed. In these lessons there was effective teaching and the students were actively engaged in purposeful learning. Students were described as being attentive, having a sense of purpose, an eagerness to learn and a positive attitude to their work. One inspection report commented:

> The students took obvious pride in what they were making, and were well able to explain and demonstrate what they were doing and why. They also took particular joy in bringing finished pieces home.

9.4.3 Atmosphere in JCSP lessons

In general there was a positive atmosphere in the lessons observed. Inspectors commented, for example, on the quality of some working environments, the attentiveness of students, the level of enthusiasm generated in lessons and the involvement of the students in these lessons. Inspectors described the quality of interaction between teachers and students in many schools as being positive and respectful. Also, there was ample evidence of positive interpersonal interactions between students. In such instances students were described as being interested in each other's work; they listened to each other, they were patient with less able classmates and they worked well together on assigned tasks. Where this occurred there was evidence of individual responses being encouraged by their teachers. Also, in many instances there was evidence of mutual respect and praise and encouragement for students on the part of the teachers.

Appropriate and positive discipline was a strong feature in the lessons observed. It was noted that students experienced an appropriate, consistent and coherent classroom code of behaviour in eighty-four per cent of the lessons observed. Here, good behaviour and progress were affirmed and inappropriate behaviour was generally dealt with consistently and fairly.

9.4.4 Teachers' expectations of students

For many students progress in learning can be gradual, while in other cases it can be painstakingly slow, and this can be frustrating for both the student and the teacher. There is a strong link between teachers' expectations and students' performance. In a programme like the JCSP, which is aimed primarily at students who have experienced little success in learning, the role that can be played by positive expectations is significant.

In some schools, students were supported in their endeavours by high expectation and encouragement from their teachers. In others the learning environment could have been enhanced by higher expectations of the students.

9.4.5 Learning

It was the view of inspectors that effective learning was taking place in the majority of the lessons observed. This was evidenced by:
- the students' work and their ability to complete a new task or recall earlier work at the end of lessons
- the high level of engagement on the part of students with lesson material
- the positive attitude of students to their work
- the relaxed and interactive but purposeful learning environment
- the quality of discussion held between students and their teachers.

It was suggested that there was "room for improvement" in students' learning in twenty-eight per cent of the lessons observed. In these instances there was either a lack of recapitulation on previous work or a lack of clarity about the purpose of the lesson, a lack of response by students, an over emphasis on rote learning, or a lack of opportunity for students to display their learning. All teaching and learning, in accordance with good practice, should have clarity of purpose, provide opportunities for students' participation and take account of student assessment outcomes.

An analysis of all of the reports on the lessons observed indicates strengths in the level of attention given by teachers to individual students, in teachers keeping lessons on target and their affirmation of students, and in the discipline systems operated. Also, it can be seen that teachers made great efforts towards enhancing students' self-esteem and self-image. The consequences of these efforts are the establishment of appropriate learning environments, where there is a high level of engagement by students and positive and appropriate discipline.

9.5 Student assessment and achievement

Profiling is the predominant student assessment tool in the JCSP. A central consideration is that the process should be continuous, particularly with regard to the monitoring and assessment of literacy and numeracy skills. Following assessment, the achievements of JCSP students are recognised through the awarding of the JCSP student profile and, following the Junior Certificate examination, the Junior Certificate.

9.5.1 Student profiling as an assessment tool

Profiling was used to record students' progress in eighty per cent of the schools that participated in this evaluation. Teachers in more than half of these schools reported that the profiling system aided planning for teaching and learning through, for example, the selection of attainable profiling statements and learning targets for students.

When surveyed, it was found that forty-seven per cent of subject teachers considered that profiling, as practised in their school, was very effective. This was the case for forty-six per cent of learning-support teachers and twenty-eight per cent of resource teachers. Practically all categories of teacher suggested, however, that profiling could be more effective if more time were made available for its implementation. It is important to note that almost ten per cent of subject teachers reported a lack of familiarity with profiling, as they were new to the JCSP. This finding raises questions with regard to how new teachers are being inducted into the programme at school level.

It was found that twenty-three per cent of subject teachers selected student profiling statements in consultation with other teachers, often in the context of JCSP team meetings. A range of practices was noted with regard to such meetings (see chapter 4, section 4.4.2). Other factors that influenced subject teachers' choice of profiling statement are listed in Table 9.4.

How are profiling statements chosen in your subject area?	Proportion of teachers
Selected in consultation with other teachers	23.0%
Appropriate to ability of students	21.6%
Teacher selects them	17.6%
Reflects Junior Certificate programme or syllabus	10.1%

Table 9.4 Factors influencing subject teachers' choice of profiling statements

Subject teachers were also asked to state how they assessed the achievement of learning targets. Table 9.5 gives the most frequent answers from 156 responses received.

How is the attainment of learning targets assessed?	Proportion of teachers
Teacher tests	38.5%
Class work	28.8%
Oral assessment	27.6%
Observation of students	10.9%
Retention of material	10.9%
Completion of assignments	10.3%
Project work	9.0%
Continuous assessment	8.3%
Homework	8.3%
Approaches involving student input	6.4%

Table 9.5   Assessment of learning targets by subject teachers

Teacher-devised tests used included Christmas and Easter examinations, modular tests (administered at mid-term, or at the end of a term), and computer-based and end-of-topic tests. Oral assessment included questioning and question-and-answer sessions, oral revision activities and group discussions. Assessment techniques that included a degree of student input were also used; these included students evaluating their own completed work, and agreements between teacher and student on the quality of work submitted.

Schools and teachers should keep the student profiling system under continual review to ensure that it is being exploited to the greatest extent possible as a mechanism for planning and student assessment.

9.5.2   Assessment of literacy

Resource and learning-support teachers played a central role in most of the schools evaluated with regard to the assessment of students' literacy skills – eighty-two per cent of learning-support teachers and sixty-eight per cent of resource teachers stated that they had responsibility in this area. Standardised tests were used to track students' progress in literacy and numeracy in more than half of the schools that participated in the evaluation. Also, three-quarters of resource and learning-support teachers reported that the outcomes of assessment influenced programme planning for their students. They also stated that students' literacy levels were taken into account when they were selecting profiling statements, and that students' literacy levels, influenced the selection of learning materials.

9.5.3   Recognition of achievement

In some schools, assessment was closely tied to rewards. The issuing of JCSP postcards was used as a form of reporting on assessment and as a way of recognising students' achievement in many schools, but in others they were not used frequently (see chapter 7, section 7.2.3). Celebration events and end-of-year presentations of profiles to students were also used as ways of rewarding achievement. It is appropriate that all JCSP schools would devise ways of continuously recognising students' effort and achievement.

9.6 Summary of findings and recommendations

9.6.1 Findings

The following is a summary of the main findings regarding the teaching and learning observed in JCSP classrooms in those schools that participated in this evaluation.

- Teachers who carefully planned lessons and employed appropriate resources were successful in engaging the attention of students and in making learning enjoyable for them.
- Planning for lessons, including the use of resources, was "optimal" or "very good" in more than eighty per cent of the JCSP lessons observed, while the appropriateness of teaching materials was considered to be "optimal" or "very good" in more than ninety per cent of lessons.
- Some teachers reported that the lack of suitable teaching materials was a serious hindrance to effective teaching in the JCSP. Teaching materials were frequently adapted to make them more suitable for use with JCSP students.
- While there was evidence of good practice in relation to the implementation of the student profiling system, this was not always so. Implementation of the system was not always co-ordinated, and its administration was seen in many instances as being cumbersome, particularly with regard to the paperwork involved and the lack of time available in which to complete it. Further, some schools did not implement profiling at all.
- Difficulties in implementing the system of profiling statements and learning targets were found to be more acute in those schools where JCSP students took some subjects in classes with non-JCSP students.
- Good practice was frequently observed in lessons with regard to the development of students' literacy and numeracy skills, as well as their social and personal skills.
- While in their questionnaire responses JCSP co-ordinators and teachers stated that they placed an emphasis on the development of literacy and numeracy skills, this was found not to be the case for the majority of lessons observed.
- Students with special educational needs were catered for through the use of special needs assistants. Students in need of learning support were catered for through team teaching and withdrawal systems. It was found that resource and learning-support teachers used the teaching approaches of the JCSP to a greater extent than other teachers.
- The inspectors reported on the extent to which teaching methods were varied and appropriate in the lessons observed. An "optimal" rating was assigned to a high proportion of these lessons, while only a small number were described as being "in need of major improvement." It was observed, however, that there was an emphasis on "teaching to the examination" in the third-year lessons of many schools.
- The adaptation by teachers of their teaching methods to suit JCSP students is prevalent throughout the programme. Many teachers reported that participation in the JCSP made a difference to the teaching methodologies they employ with non-JCSP classes.
- Students' participation in lessons was heavily influenced by the attention given to individual students by teachers and by the degree of involvement of each student in their own learning.
- Insufficient attention was given to monitoring attendance and punctuality. There was no evidence of attendance being monitored in thirty-one per cent of lessons observed.
- Profiling was used to assess students' progress in eighty per cent of the schools that participated in this evaluation.
- Standardised tests were used to track students' progress in literacy and numeracy in more than half of the schools that participated in the evaluation. Resource and learning-support teachers play a central role in most schools with regard to the assessment of these skills.

9.6.2   Recommendations

The following recommendations are made with regard to the teaching and learning process as it affects the JCSP.

Recommendations for schools

- Schools should be cognisant of the textbooks and other resources that they use with JCSP students and ensure that they are appropriate to the students' needs, interests and ability levels. The subjects, themes and language of textbooks, for example, should be appropriate to students' age and ability levels.
- The profiling system should be planned, organised and co-ordinated to ensure that there is a consistent approach to it by relevant staff. Profiling should be used to inform planning for teaching and learning, and it should be implemented with all students in the JCSP.
- Greater attention needs to be given to the development of both literacy and numeracy skills in the classroom. This emphasis should permeate all areas of the JCSP. Also, the personal and social development of students should be prioritised in all lessons, with use being made of appropriate profiling statements.
- Evidence of students' progress, including the achievement of learning targets, should be accessible to students, teachers, and parents alike.
- Planning for students with special educational needs should involve subject and specialist teachers.
- Greater attention needs to be given to monitoring students' attendance and punctuality in lessons. Schools should devise a system of centrally administering attendance and punctuality data and communicating it with the home.
- All teaching and learning in the JCSP should have clarity of purpose, provide opportunities for students' participation and take account of student assessment outcomes.
- The outcomes of assessment should inform the selection of profiling statements and learning targets. Students should be made aware of their progress in all subject areas.
- Schools should devise ways of continuously recognising students' effort and achievement.

Recommendations for policy-makers and policy advisers

- Teaching methodologies need to be tailored more to the needs and interests of students. Teachers should be supported in this task by a whole-school emphasis on quality in teaching and learning. The JCSP Support Service can play an important role in this area.

10 Does the JCSP Make a Difference?

Outcomes of the JCSP

10.1 Introduction

Where the JCSP operates alongside a different programme, but one that has similar aims and objectives to the JCSP (e.g., the SCP – see Chapter 2, Section 2.2) it can sometimes prove difficult to attribute outcomes exclusively to either the JCSP or to that other programme. Notwithstanding this, according to information gleaned from interviews and discussions held with, and questionnaire responses received from, relevant JCSP school personnel, including school principals, JCSP co-ordinators, subject teachers, HSCL teachers and learning-support and resource teachers, a picture of a range of outcomes of the JCSP emerged in the schools evaluated. Other sources of evidence included interviews with students, inspection reports and data held by the Department of Education and Science and the State Examinations Commission with regard to JCSP students' performance in the Junior Certificate examination.

It was reported by the various school personnel that the JCSP contributes towards enhanced:
- attendance and retention
- motivation and attitude
- literacy and numeracy achievement
- social skills
- performance in the Junior Certificate examination
- progression after the Junior Certificate

This chapter looks at each of these areas in turn. It concludes by referring to a number of other outcomes that impinge on the school, individual teachers and the wider community.

10.2 Attendance and retention

An evaluation of the outcomes of the JCSP must address the success or otherwise of the programme at keeping students in school, at least until the end of the junior cycle. When surveyed, HSCL and SCP co-ordinators, as well as learning-support, resource and subject teachers cited improved attendance and retention as one valuable outcome of the programme. The ratings of 224 respondents are summarised in Table 10.1.

	HSCL co-ordinators (n = 17)	Learning-support teachers (n = 20)	Resource teachers (n = 21)	Subject teachers (n = 149)	SCP co-ordinators (n = 17)
Significant Impact	47.1%	25.0%	57.1%	57.0%	76.5%
Moderate Impact	47.1%	70.0%	38.1%	28.9%	23.5%
Slight Impact	5.9%	5.0%	4.8%	11.4%	0
No Impact	0	0	0	2.7%	0

Table 10.1 Proportion of questionnaire respondents reporting the impact of the JCSP on attendance and retention

It is noteworthy that almost all categories of teachers stated that the programme had a "significant" or "moderate" impact on attendance and retention. This is in keeping with the information supplied to the inspectors during discussions in the schools. In one school, for example, the guidance counsellor estimated that the number of students staying on to senior cycle in their school, and completing it, had trebled in the last few years. While it was not suggested that this was entirely due to the JCSP, it was clear, according to the guidance counsellor, that the JCSP had played its part in encouraging students to stay in school longer than was the case.

Further, when JCSP co-ordinators were invited to list three benefits of the programme thirty per cent listed improved retention rates. Co-ordinators frequently commented that in the absence of the JCSP students would most probably have left school without formal qualifications, and cited a reduction in the number of their early school leavers as one of the results of the programme.

Inspectors commented on the issue of student retention in twenty-five out of thirty school inspection reports. In nineteen of these reports it was commented that there was evidence that the JCSP was having a positive impact on retention levels. In two reports the inspectors noted that while the attendance of JCSP students was quite good, their punctuality was less consistent, while four reports made reference to poor student attendance at school.

While it might be assumed that the retention of students should be easy to evaluate schools generally did not keep specific data on the attendance and retention rates of their JCSP students. This absence of hard numerical data was an obstacle to definitively evaluating the success of the programme at improving retention. More definitive judgements on the impact of the programme at retaining students in school would have been possible if appropriate attendance and retention records had been available to support teachers' impressions.

In order to evaluate effectively the impact of the JCSP on student retention and attendance schools should maintain and analyse data regarding student retention. The JCSP Support Service and/or the National Education Welfare Board (NEWB) could play a role in aggregating such records on a national basis.

10.3   Motivation and attitude

A reported outcome of the JCSP in practically all schools evaluated was a notable improvement in students' motivation and in their attitude to school. This was particularly evident in questionnaire responses, student interviews and school inspection reports.

Table 10.2, based on a total of 214 questionnaire responses, indicates that the majority of teachers reported that the JCSP improved students' motivation significantly.

	Learning-support teachers (n = 20)	Resource teachers (n = 22)	Subject teachers (n = 154)	SCP co-ordinators (n = 18)
Significant Impact	70.0%	68.2%	57.1%	61.1%
Moderate Impact	25.0%	27.3%	33.8%	38.9%
Slight Impact	5.0%	4.5%	6.5%	0
No Impact	0	0	2.6%	0

Table 10.2   Proportion of questionnaire respondents reporting the impact of the JCSP on motivation

When invited to give details of how the JCSP had improved students' motivation, SCP co-ordinators referred to the fact that it provides achievable goals and targets. They also referred to the manageability of students' workload within the JCSP. Other responses included:

   "Students want to give themselves the credit they are due"

   "Individual programmes mean that students have a chance to succeed"

   "Students feel they can do the homework"

   "The JCSP curriculum is suited to students"

   "There is greater perceived support from the JCSP co-ordinator"

   "Students' self-esteem improves because they are doing the JCSP"

   "Students can see progress: they don't have to wait for Christmas or summer exams"

   "Students get involved in other projects and competitions as a result of involvement in the JCSP"

   "Students receive more personal attention"

   "There are award systems within the JCSP"

The following extract from one inspection report reflects the positive effect of the JCSP on students' attitude:

   From classroom observation and from the structured interview with third-year students it is evident that the attitude of the students towards their schooling and to their involvement in the programme is positive. The students presented as content and confident, open and friendly and with a strong sense of group identity. Satisfactory attendance levels among the JCSP classes attest to their positive disposition towards the programme.

In schools where JCSP was effectively implemented inspectors were able to corroborate reports of improvements to student motivation and attitude from school personnel and students themselves during their structured interviews with students, as well as during visits to classrooms. At the student interviews, for example, students spoke confidently about their experience of the JCSP, they approached the interviews with a sense of maturity and were keen to communicate to inspectors the type and extent of the work that they had done as part of their JCSP. It is noteworthy that on many occasions students mentioned numerous initiatives of the JCSP as a source of interest and motivation for them at school, e.g., Make-a-Book, Readalong, Fusebox, peer tutoring, library initiatives and celebrations. In over seventy-five per cent of lessons visited by inspectors students were reported to be enjoying their work, or displaying a positive attitude to the JCSP in general. The majority of students were attentive and eager to learn and the quality of teacher-student and student-student relationships observed in lessons was respectful.

The JCSP is successful at engaging the majority of students, and hence at encouraging them to continue with their schooling. The nature and structure of the programme, including its many initiatives, coupled with the implementation by schools of positive discipline programmes, generally succeeds at motivating students and fosters in them a positive attitude to their schooling. School management, JCSP co-ordinators, subject and specialist teachers, should endeavour, in accordance with best practice, to regularly elicit the views of their students regarding the programme they offer them. This could be done by including students in the review of a school's programme.

10.4   Literacy and numeracy

A feature of the JCSP target group of students is that difficulties with literacy and numeracy interfere with their ability to cope with the normal demands of school and everyday life. Given the emphasis on the development of literacy and numeracy skills in the JCSP it can be taken that one outcome of an effective programme should be an improvement in the literacy and numeracy skills of its students. In the absence of standardised results comparable between schools, the main source of evidence for the existence, or otherwise, of this outcome was the questionnaire responses of the learning-support and resource teachers, as well as subject teachers. These teachers were best placed to offer comment on the impact of the JCSP on the literacy and numeracy skills of students.

Learning-support teachers, resource teachers and subject teachers were asked to rate participation in the JCSP according to its contribution to the development of students' literacy and numeracy skills. The results are given in Table 10.3.

	Learning-support teachers (n = 19)		Resource teachers (n = 21)	(n = 19)	Subject teachers (n = 141)	(n = 137)
	Literacy	Numeracy	Literacy	Numeracy	Literacy	Numeracy
Significant Impact	78.9%	63.2%	66.7%	63.2%	48.2%	43.9%
Moderate Impact	21.1%	36.8%	33.3%	36.8%	41.8%	42.4%
Slight Impact	0	0	0	0	9.2%	12.1%
No Impact	0	0	0	0	0.7%	1.5%

Table 10.3 Proportion of questionnaire respondents reporting the impact of the JCSP on literacy and numeracy skills

All learning-support teachers surveyed said that the JCSP was effective at improving students' literacy skills stating that it had either a 'significant impact' or a 'moderate impact' on the development of these skills. Further, learning-support teachers reported that the learning support provided in the JCSP was by far the greatest factor that contributed to an improvement in literacy skills. Other contributing factors endorsed by learning-support teachers included the availability of statements and clearly defined goals for reading, small classes and extra resources. These teachers also endorsed a number of strategies specific to the teaching of reading, e.g., Make-a-Book, paired reading and Readalong. A small team of JCSP teachers in a school, and the teaching of fewer subjects to students (i.e., a reduced curriculum but not a reduced timetable) were also considered to play a role in the development of students' literacy skills.

It is significant that subject teachers did not rate the benefits to either literacy or numeracy as highly as did specialist teachers. Perhaps parallels can be drawn here to the findings from inspection visits to JCSP lessons where it was observed that forty-five per cent of lessons were rated poorly with regard to their attention to literacy and numeracy.

All three categories of teachers rated the benefits to literacy more highly than the benefits to numeracy. This finding is in keeping with inspection reports, which referred to the fact that, in general, more attention was given to the development of literacy skills than to numeracy skills in most if not all of those lessons visited. Parallels can be drawn here with the findings of the PISA study (2005). These show that the literacy skills of Irish second-level students are generally better than their numeracy skills.[13]

Overall, from the survey findings, it can be said that all categories of teacher view the JCSP as having a positive impact on the development of students' literacy and numeracy skills, but especially on literacy skills. To accurately measure the impact of the JCSP on literacy and numeracy levels, consideration should be given to the use of regular standardised testing in all schools participating in the programme.

10.5   Social skills

Given the emphasis on the development of students' social and personal development in the JCSP it can be taken that an outcome of an effective programme should be an improvement in students' personal and social skills. The JCSP fosters social and personal skills, as examined in section 8.4.3, in a variety of ways. The predominant methods used are cross-curricular statements, celebration events and out-of-school activities. Learning-support and resource teachers, as well as SCP co-ordinators, were asked to indicate the extent to which students' social skills had benefited from their participation in the JCSP. Table 10.4 gives details of 206 responses.

---

13   The second cycle of the Programme for International Student Assessment (PISA, 2003) took place in thirty OECD member-countries and eleven non-OECD countries. However, the response from one OECD country was too low to ensure reliable achievement estimates, and so comparisons were made for twenty-nine rather than thirty OECD countries. The study involved the assessment of students' knowledge and skills in four domains: mathematics, reading literacy, science, and cross-curricular problem-solving. Irish students achieved a mean score of 502.8 on the combined mathematics scale (OECD mean score: 500.0) and ranked twentieth out of the forty participating countries. Irish students achieved a mean score of 515.5 on the reading literacy scale (OECD mean score: 494.2) and ranked seventh out of the forty participating countries.

	Learning-support teachers (n = 19)	Resource teachers (n = 22)	Subject teachers (n = 149)	SCP co-ordinators (n = 16)
Significant	63.2%	68.2%	59.1%	56.3%
Moderate	36.8%	31.8%	33.6%	37.5%
Slight	0	0	6.0	6.3%
None	0	0	1.3	0

Table 10.4 Proportion of respondents reporting the impact of the JCSP on social skills

The majority of all categories of respondents expressed the view that the JCSP had made either a 'significant' or 'moderate' impact on developing students' social skills.

It was found that schools that participated in the SCP, and other such initiatives such as the SSRI, often organised clubs or other activities to promote personal and social development. SCP co-ordinators were invited to suggest ways in which the JCSP had assisted in developing good student-student relations. Some of their comments included:

"Students help each other to reach self-set targets"

"There is less competition among students because of individual programmes"

"Students work well together"

"More personal development type work is covered in the JCSP"

"More group and teamwork takes place in lessons"

"Smaller class/group sizes in the JCSP allow for more interaction"

"There are opportunities for teamwork in every subject area"

"By second year, students usually co-operate well and care for each other"

"Co-operation and group work improve social skills"

"The focus on cross-curricular development enhances social and personal skills"

"Skills modeled and learned are more easily retained and used in small-group settings"

"Peer-tutoring in the JCSP, involving first and third year students, has promoted improved relationships"

SCP co-ordinators were also asked to state the extent to which the JCSP assisted in developing good teacher-student interactions and relations. Of the sixteen co-ordinators that responded more than two-thirds reported that it had helped "very much," while more than a quarter stated that it had helped to a "moderate" degree. Some of their comments included:

"Small class sizes help"

"Discussions in smaller classes/groups lead to better relationships"

"Students' work is acknowledged at all stages of completion – this helps foster good relationships between teachers and students"

"Students see teachers as being helpful and interested"

"The less formal yet practical approach leads to better teacher-student relationships"

"Meaningful activities lead to improved teacher-student relationships"

"The JCSP allows teachers and students to share students' learning"

"Practical, relevant activities (e.g., local history) help"

"Students develop more open relationships with teachers, allowing for greater productivity"

"Students believe an extra effort is being made for them so they are more receptive to help"

It is difficult to measure accurately the impact of the JCSP on students' social skills. Notwithstanding this, from inspectors' observations of and interactions with students during the course of this evaluation, and from feedback received from the various JCSP personnel in schools, it can be stated with some degree of confidence that the JCSP is successful at enhancing students' personal and social development. This issue was discussed in Chapter 8, section 8.4.3, and the recommendation was made that the development of students' social skills should continue to be a main emphasis of the JCSP curriculum. Further, given the significance to students of the nature of interactions between teachers and students, as well as the fact that all teachers are be able to contribute to the development of students social and personal skills, all JCSP staff, but especially the JCSP teaching team, should be involved in choosing and awarding to students' the social and personal development profiling statements.

10.6   The Junior Certificate examination

Analysing JCSP students' examination results is another means that can be used to gain an impression of the impact that the JCSP has on students. It is a stated goal of the programme to support students in completing the junior cycle, and achieve success in at least a restricted number of subjects in the Junior Certificate examination. Given that individual student achievement is recorded by means of the profiling process, a student who does not sit the examination will still be awarded an officially certified record of academic and cross-curricular achievement. However, for many students, sitting the state examination can be an achievement in itself, irrespective of the grades achieved.

In their questionnaire, JCSP co-ordinators were asked to state whether or not JCSP students in their school usually sat the Junior Certificate examination. The majority of co-ordinators – just over sixty per cent – stated that their students "always" sit the examination, close on twenty-seven per cent of co-ordinators stated that students "usually" do, nearly eight per cent of co-ordinators stated that students "sometimes" do, while just under four per cent of co-ordinators stated that students "never" do. These responses are borne out by a comparison between the number of JCSP students studying various subjects and the number who sit the Junior Certificate examination in the same subjects. The comparison for the academic year 2002/2003 and the 2003 Junior Certificate examination can be seen in Table 10.5. It is noteworthy that the science and language subjects predominantly feature at the bottom end of this table indicating that they are the less popular examinations taken by JCSP students. This issue is examined in some depth in Chapter 8.

Some inspection reports commented on the good results achieved by JCSP students in the Junior Certificate examination. One, for example, noted that many JCSP students achieved above-average results compared with other Junior Certificate classes in their school. Another noted:

> Teachers are understandably proud of the examination outcomes achieved by many JCSP students. Some subject teachers reported pass rates of up to 100 per cent at Foundation and Ordinary levels in recent years.

Although it is difficult to equate success in the Junior Certificate examination with participation in the JCSP there are indicators, based predominantly on the views of JCSP personnel in schools, that the JCSP is successful at keeping students, who might otherwise have left, in school up to the end of the junior cycle. This achievement itself brings students face to face with the Junior Certificate examination and so in many respects encourages them to sit the examination and achieve in it.

Subject	Number of Students Enrolled	Number of Students Examined	Proportion Examined
Environmental and Social Studies (ESS)	287	259	90.2%
English	1518	1332	87.7%
Business studies	369	321	87.0%
Home economics	822	707	86.0%
Materials technology (wood)	732	611	83.5%
Geography	824	667	80.9%
Art, craft, and design	1156	927	80.2%
Technical graphics	253	203	80.2%
Mathematics	1513	1334	79.8%
History	792	632	79.8%
Metalwork	662	521	78.7%
Civic, social and political education	1474	1131	76.7%
Italian	88	66	75.0%
Science	701	515	73.5%
German	23	16	69.6%
Irish	1302	877	67.4%
French	216	134	62.0%
Technology	48	26	54.2%
Spanish	36	18	50.0%
Music	180	83	46.1%
Typewriting	44	15	34.1%

Table 10.5   Comparison between number of JCSP students studying subjects and exam "sits" in those subjects, 2002/2003

The most common choice for those students who stay on in school after the JCSP is the Leaving Certificate Applied (LCA), followed by the Transition Year programme, the Leaving Certificate Vocational Programme (LCVP), and the established Leaving Certificate, in that order. In structured interviews held as part of this evaluation, students were asked what they planned to do after their Junior Certificate. It was found that in most schools approximately half of the students intended staying on to pursue the senior cycle (mainly to do the LCA), while the remainder spoke of leaving to enter employment or to undertake an apprenticeship[14]. The number of JCSP students who stay in school after the JCSP is lower

---

14   Progression to an apprenticeship programme is dependent on results achieved in the Junior Certificate examination. Students must achieve a minimum of five grade D's in this examination to be eligible for entry to an apprenticeship.

than that for the general cohort of junior cycle students. Notwithstanding this, the proportion staying in school after their Junior Certificate is showing a steady increase from year to year. Table 10.6 shows the progression of three cohorts of JCSP students: those who took their Junior Certificate examination in 2001, 2002, and 2003. The data is based on information held by the Department of Education and Science.

	Year		
	2001 (n = 1,007)	2002 (n = 1,224)	2003 (n = 1,518)
Leaving Certificate Applied	42.2%	44.9%	46.1%
Transition year programme	13.4%	14.9%	14.6%
LCVP, year 1	9.4%	7.1%	9.7%
Established Leaving Certificate	7.0%	8.5%	7.4%
VPTP II, year 1	0.1%	0.2%	0.2%
JCSP, year 3	1.5%	0.9%	0.7%
JCSP, year 2	0	0	0.1%
Junior Certificate, year 3	0.2%	0.2%	0.3%
Junior Certificate, year 2	0	0.1%	0
Data not available	26.2%	23.2%	20.9%
Total proportion still in school	73.8%	76.8%	79.1%

Table 10.6 Progression of JCSP students after the Junior Certificate

The row entitled *"Data not available"* refers to students who left school after their Junior Certificate. No data is available regarding the destination of these students, but would, most likely, include those students who progressed to employment and apprenticeship. The relatively high percentages here, however, does raise questions regarding the success, or otherwise, of the JCSP at encouraging students to stay on at school after their Junior Certificate. The recommendation has already been made (see Chapter 7, section 7.4) that schools should track all JCSP students' progression after completion of the junior cycle. This would assist in compiling a comprehensive picture of the progression routes of students after they complete the JCSP.

10.7   Benefits of the JCSP to school, teachers, and community

In addition to the outcomes already discussed, JCSP personnel frequently referred to other beneficial effects of the JCSP during the course of the evaluation. It was mentioned, for example, that the programme contributed to enhanced home-school-community links. The following are some responses of the HSCL co-ordinator.

> *"Some JCSP tasks or activities link to the community to a greater extent than activities associated with the traditional junior cycle programme"*

> *"The JCSP means that students with special needs do not have to leave the area to go to school elsewhere"*

> *"Most parents are understanding of the JCSP when given an opportunity to discuss its goals and appreciate the benefits for their children"*

> *"There is an increased awareness in the community of the efforts of schools to meet the needs of many learners who were not catered for in the past"*

> *"The successful integration of students into the community is achieved as a result of the wide range of community agencies involved in providing the JCSP"*
>
> *"Student profiles help prospective employers"*
>
> *"The JCSP meets the needs of students and so forges strong relations between school and home, and between school and community"*

JCSP personnel also reported that the programme creates an environment for students where they can enjoy their learning. It was reported that the JCSP allowed for a recognition and celebration of students' achievement not normally associated with mainstream programmes in post-primary schools. From the teachers' viewpoint the programme not only provides a clear structure or framework for teaching and learning but can also contribute towards the enhancement of teaching methods. JCSP teachers also tend to engage more in teamwork in schools.

10.8   Summary of findings and recommendations

10.8.1 Findings

The following is a summary of the main findings with regard to the outcomes of the JCSP in those schools that participated in this evaluation.

- It was reported by various JCSP school personnel that the programme contributed to enhanced student attendance and retention at school. In the absence of relevant concrete data it is difficult to corroborate this finding. Notwithstanding this, in the majority of schools that participated in this evaluation there was evidence to suggest that the JCSP was having a positive impact on student retention levels. In the majority of cases this was because of the many strategies that schools had put in place to closely monitor attendance and punctuality. A small number of inspection reports, however, made reference to poor student attendance and punctuality.

- It was reported by JCSP school personnel that the programme contributed to enhanced literacy and numeracy skills among students. JCSP co-ordinators and teachers reported placing an emphasis on the development of literacy and numeracy skills in JCSP lessons. However, this did not hold true for the 108 lessons observed and rated for attention to literacy and numeracy.

- JCSP personnel reported that the programme contributed towards enhanced student motivation and attitude towards their schooling, and also towards developing their social skills. In the main, inspections corroborated these reports following their discussions and interactions with students.

- There are indicators, based predominantly on the views of schools' JCSP personnel, but also on data held by the Department of Education and Science and SEC, that the JCSP is successful at retaining in school students who might have otherwise left before the end of their junior cycle. This brings students face to face with the Junior Certificate examination and so can encourage them to sit the examination and achieve in it. The majority of students sat all or most of their subjects in their Junior Certificate examination.

- JCSP personnel reported that the programme contributed to enhanced home-school-community links; that it provided opportunities for students to enjoy and celebrate their learning; it encouraged the use of varied and alternative teaching strategies; and it encouraged teamwork among members of the teaching staff in schools.

10.8.2 Recommendations

The following recommendations are made with regard to improving the quality of the outcome of the JCSP in schools.

Recommendations for schools

- In order to effectively evaluate the impact of the JCSP on student retention and attendance it is important that individual schools maintain detailed records regarding student enrolments and engage in their own analysis of these data.
- Schools should track the destination of JCSP students who do not progress to the senior cycle. This information could also be used to assess the success, or otherwise, of the programme.
- Schools should endeavour, in accordance with best practice, to regularly elicit the views of their students regarding the programme they offer them. This could be done by including students in the review of a school's programme.
- Given the significance to students of the nature of interactions between teachers and students, as well as the fact that all teachers are be able to contribute to the development of students' social and personal skills, all JCSP staff, but especially the JCSP teaching team, should be involved in choosing and awarding to students the social and personal development profiling statements.
- To measure the impact of the JCSP on students' literacy and numeracy, consideration should be given to regular use of standardised tests by schools participating in the programme.

Recommendations for policy-makers and policy advisers

- The development of students' social skills should continue to be a main emphasis of the JCSP.

11 JCSP Evaluation: The Lessons

Summary of findings and recommendations

11.1 Introduction

This chapter brings together all the findings and recommendations already referred to throughout this report. The findings show that, while the JCSP is succeeding and thriving in many schools, there are also a number of areas of the programme that need to be further developed and expanded. The recommendations made are divided into two categories: those relating to schools and those relating to policy.

Many recommendations are directed at schools. The school Principal, the JCSP co-ordinator, the HSCL co-ordinator, the learning-support teacher, the resource teacher and individual JCSP subject teachers can all play a role in their implementation. Schools could also seek to involve the whole school community, such as parents and local employers and industry, where possible. Schools should adopt a strategic approach to implementing the recommendations of this report. This could involve, for example, undertaking an initial assessment of their own JCSP to determine those aspects of the programme that warrant priority for immediate action. This approach would allow schools to give priority to recommendations for action. In implementing the following recommendations, schools should seek advice and support from the JCSP Support Service, where applicable.

The second category of recommendations is directed at policy advisers and policy-makers. This includes such bodies as the Department of Education and Science, the National Council for Curriculum and Assessment, the National Council for Special Education, the National Educational Psychological Service, and the relevant support services. The adoption of these recommendations would support schools in their endeavours to implement the recommendations specifically aimed at schools.

The sections that follow are concerned with each of the main areas of the programme evaluated, all of which have already been described in the different chapters of this report. Each of these sections should be read in the context of the relevant chapter. Each contains the main findings related to that area of the programme evaluated, followed by the appropriate recommendations aimed at schools as well as those aimed at policy-makers and policy advisers.

11.2   Organisation of the JCSP in schools

11.2.1 Findings

- The frequency of JCSP team meetings in schools varies considerably: approximately twenty per cent of schools held no JCSP meetings during the school year.
- The majority of JCSP schools do not have appropriate record-keeping systems in place.
- The large size of the teaching team in the majority of schools is not in accordance with guidelines on JCSP and may not be in the best interest of the programme.
- There is wide variation in schools regarding the practice of student profiling. In most schools there was little involvement by students in the process.
- The student profiling system makes considerable time and administration demands on schools.
- For most schools the necessity to provide JCSP students with additional teaching time in Mathematics and English is an important consideration.
- While there is a good level of informal review of the JCSP in schools formal review of the programme takes place in only a minority of schools.

11.2.2 Recommendations for schools

- Each school should have a JCSP planning group that includes the principal, the JCSP co-ordinator, and representatives of the school's JCSP teaching team. Planning for the programme in a school should include curriculum, assessment, resources, student selection and staffing. Schools should also allocate time for meetings to plan and run the JCSP. Each school should document its JCSP.
- Schools should ensure that formal and informal review takes place so as to ensure that the programme continues to meet the needs of students.
- Schools, with the aid of the support service where necessary, should plan and implement systems, including the use of ICT, for the preparation, storage, updating and retention of JCSP records.
- Schools should keep their JCSP teaching teams as small as practicable, consistent with having enough team members with the range of skills necessary to provide an effective programme.
- Mathematics and English lessons should be timetabled, as far as possible, to be taught during the morning so as to enhance the effectiveness of the provision for literacy and numeracy within the JCSP.
- Profiling should be implemented in each school's JCSP. The selection and assessment of profiling statements should be co-ordinated and student involvement should be facilitated.
- Each school's JCSP criteria for selection of students should be documented. Records should indicate how each student is expected to benefit from the JCSP and these should be retained in the school.

11.2.3 Recommendations for policy-makers and policy advisers

- The JCSP student profiling system should be subjected to a thorough review with a view to exploring ways of reducing the administrative requirement of the programme on schools. Training should be provided to enable co-ordinators and teachers to implement profiling efficiently through an increased use of ICT, including the development of suitable software for this purpose.

11.3   Resources

11.3.1 Findings

- Appropriate co-ordination is necessary for the effective implementation of the JCSP. Schools typically use between two and four hours a week of the additional teaching time allocation for JCSP co-ordination activities. Difficulties arise in co-ordination when there is an inappropriate allocation of co-ordination time. It was found that difficulties in the co-ordination of the programme and the profiling of students were exacerbated as the number of students in the JCSP increased.

- It is the view of JCSP co-ordinators that the funds provided for the programme by the Department of Education and Science do not adequately meet the needs of providing an effective JCSP in a school. For most schools this funding is supplemented by funds from other sources.

- A low proportion of JCSP personnel, other than co-ordinators, participated in relevant ICD courses in the two years prior to this evaluation. Of those who did participate, there was a high degree of satisfaction with the quality of the courses attended.

- Some schools experience difficulty in accessing relevant ICD courses.

11.3.2 Recommendations for schools

- Where programmes with similar objectives to those of the JCSP operate in a school, such as the SCP, the school should ensure that such programmes are co-ordinated with the JCSP so as to maximise the benefits to students.

- Schools should assess staff needs, and in turn plan for appropriate participation in relevant JCSP in-career development courses as part of their development planning process.

11.3.3 Recommendations for policy-makers and policy advisers

- At present an additional allocation of 0.25 teachers (or 5.5 hours per week) for each forty-five students enrolled is provided to schools. Given the significant workload involved in co-ordinating the JCSP, particularly in those schools where large numbers of JCSP students are enrolled, consideration should be given to revising the additional whole-time teacher equivalent allocation currently made available to schools.

- Consideration needs to be given to providing special schools with some additional allocation of teaching time.

- The funding arrangements currently in place for the JCSP should be reviewed and should be considered in light of funding made available for other initiatives and programmes in schools.

- The JCSP Support Service should undertake a review of the strategies employed in the delivery of ICD provision associated with the programme. There is also a need for more in-career development courses in the area of special educational needs.

11.4   Student selection procedures

11.4.1 Findings

- Academic attainment, as reflected in students' assessment results on entry to post-primary school, is the principal criterion by which most schools select students for the JCSP.
- Not all schools involve primary schools and parents in student selection procedures.
- The JCSP, with its curricular independence and cross-curricular and short-term targets, seems well suited to meeting the needs of students with special educational needs, while at the same time meeting the needs of its original target group.
- The shorter school day in special schools makes it more difficult to implement the JCSP.

11.4.2 Recommendations for schools

- Schools should develop and foster an awareness of the benefits of the JCSP among parents and primary schools through such means as visits to primary schools, open days and information evenings.
- The selection of students for JCSP should include:
  - the involvement of senior management and the JCSP team
  - liaison between primary and post-primary schools at an early stage
  - the involvement of parents in the selection process
  - use by schools of a wider range of recognised indicators of risk of early school leaving
  - ensuring that any assessment tools used are appropriate, up-to-date, norm-referenced and culturally fair
- There should be follow-up by schools to the initial assessment carried out. This would ensure that all students who might benefit from the JCSP can continue to participate in the programme, while those who might no longer require the support of the JCSP can avail of the opportunity to follow the mainstream Junior Certificate programme.

11.4.3 Recommendations for policy-makers and policy advisers

- The JCSP Support Service, in consultation with NEPS, should develop and disseminate appropriate guidelines to schools on best practice for the selection of students for the JCSP, including the assessment instruments to be used.
- Consideration should be given to how JCSP can best continue to meet the needs of post-primary students with special education needs. The Special Education Support Service (SESS) and the JCSP Support Service, in collaboration with other relevant stakeholders, should be asked to address this issue.

11.5   Participation and retention

11.5.1 Findings

- Some schools have been resourceful and innovative in overcoming the reluctance of parents to engage with schools and with the JCSP, others have not been so successful.
- Although JCSP postcards can have a beneficial effect on JCSP students in building their self-esteem and helping to predispose them positively towards school, not all schools make use of them.
- While guidance and counselling play a significant role in the JCSP provided by many schools, in nearly one-third of the schools inspectors recommended a role, or a greater role, for guidance.
- Currently, much evidence on the improvements in students' attendance and retention is anecdotal.

11.5.2 Recommendations for schools

- Schools should foster regular contact between home and school and all teachers should use JCSP postcards in a systematic way.
- Schools should adopt a positive discipline approach in their code of student behaviour.
- Schools should develop and implement a pastoral care policy or strategy for JCSP students.
- Schools should provide JCSP students with guidance, including career advice, and counselling.
- Schools should implement effective systems for recording and monitoring attendance and punctuality in the JCSP.

11.5.3 Recommendations for policy-makers and policy advisers

- Guidelines on the provision of guidance and counselling within the JCSP should be further developed for schools.
- School records of students' attendance and their destination after completing the junior cycle should be aggregated nationally in order to more accurately determine the success of the JCSP at improving attendance and retention.

11.6 The JCSP curriculum

11.6.1 Findings

- Schools do not always consider students' abilities, or have a team approach, when developing their JCSP curriculum.
- JCSP students did not take a reduced number of Junior Certificate examination subjects in a significant number of the thirty schools that participated in the evaluation.
- Well over half of the schools that participated in the evaluation did not provide students with science, Irish or modern European languages as part of their curriculum. With regard to languages, for example, the proportion was as high as eighty per cent. In general, schools felt that the curriculum associated with these subjects was not appropriate for JCSP students.
- Practical subjects meet a wide range of students' needs and aspirations and so tend to enhance the general quality of the programme for students.
- There is a great variety of practice with regard to the use of ICT in the JCSP. However, in a significant number of schools JCSP students did not engage with ICT.
- At the time of the evaluation no school had a written whole-school literacy or numeracy policy in place. In general it was found that the development of students' literacy and numeracy skills was considered to be within the remit of English and Mathematics or technology-based lessons only.
- The JCSP is successful at enhancing students' personal and social development. It was evident that students' self-esteem had benefited from participation in the JCSP.
- Most schools placed a strong emphasis on cross-curricular activity, including the organisation of musicals or concerts, mini-company work and Christmas celebrations.
- Withdrawing students from certain lessons was the principal method for organising learning support in almost all schools.

11.6.2 Recommendations for schools

- School management and staff should work closely together when developing their JCSP curriculum. Also, the curriculum should be tailored to meet the needs and abilities of individual students.
- Schools should exploit the possibilities presented by ICT in both the administration of the programme and in learning and teaching.

- Irish Cultural Studies courses should supplement, and not replace, the study of Irish in the JCSP. Where relevant, schools should review the place of Irish Cultural Studies in their JCSP curriculum and give consideration to including foundation level Junior Certificate Irish.
- The practice by some schools of shortening the school day for JCSP students should be discontinued.
- Each school providing the JCSP should develop a whole-school literacy strategy. Attention should be given to the differing literacy needs of students in the teaching of the curriculum. All teachers should take responsibility for the development of literacy in their subject areas and schools should undertake whole-school staff development in this area.
- Each school providing the JCSP should develop a whole-school numeracy strategy. There should be a whole-school approach to numeracy throughout the programme, and this should be kept under continuous review. Diagnostic testing, which is used to determine students' numeracy levels, their needs, and their progress in numeracy development, should be used more frequently by schools.
- The development of students' social and personal skills should continue to be an emphasis of the JCSP.

11.6.3 Recommendations for policy-makers and policy advisers

- It has been recommended earlier in this report that consideration should be given to how the JCSP can best continue to meet the needs of post-primary students with special educational needs. Areas that warrant consideration here include:
  - personnel from mainstream schools that provide the JCSP as well as personnel from those schools that have students with special educational needs, and personnel from special schools that provide the JCSP, should come together to share insights, ideas, and methods
  - a greater range of student profiling statements throughout all subjects should be developed; also the language used in profiling statements should be clear and easily understood.
- The NCCA, in collaboration with the JCSP Support Service, should develop and support the implementation of suitable programmes in modern European languages for the JCSP.
- The JCSP Support Service should investigate how the use of ICT in the JCSP could be substantially developed in order to support teaching and learning.

11.7   Teaching and learning

11.7.1 Findings

- Teachers who carefully planned lessons and employed appropriate resources were successful in engaging the attention of students and in making learning enjoyable for them.
- Planning for lessons, including the use of resources, was "optimal" or "very good" in more than eighty per cent of the JCSP lessons observed, while the appropriateness of teaching materials was considered to be "optimal" or "very good" in more than ninety per cent of lessons.
- Some teachers reported that the lack of suitable teaching materials was a serious hindrance to effective teaching in the JCSP. Teaching materials were frequently adapted to make them more suitable for use with JCSP students.
- While there was evidence of good practice in relation to the implementation of the student profiling system, this was not always so. Implementation of the system was not always co-ordinated, and its administration was seen in many instances as being cumbersome, particularly with regard to the paperwork involved and the lack of time available in which to complete it. Some schools did not implement profiling at all.

- Difficulties in implementing the system of profiling statements and learning targets were found to be more acute in those schools where JCSP students took some subjects in classes with non-JCSP students.
- Good practice was frequently observed in lessons with regard to the development of students' literacy and numeracy skills, as well as their social and personal skills.
- While in their questionnaire responses JCSP co-ordinators and teachers stated that they placed an emphasis on the development of literacy and numeracy skills, this was found not to be the case for the majority of lessons observed.
- Students with special educational needs were supported by special needs assistants in most cases. Students in need of learning support were catered for through team teaching and withdrawal systems. It was found that resource and learning-support teachers used the teaching approaches of the JCSP to a greater extent than other teachers.
- The inspectors reported on the extent to which teaching methods were varied and appropriate in the lessons observed. An "optimal" rating was assigned to a high proportion of these lessons, while only a small number were described as being "in need of major improvement." It was observed, however, that there was an emphasis on "teaching to the examination" in the third-year lessons of many schools.
- The adaptation by teachers of their teaching methods to suit JCSP students is prevalent throughout the programme. Many teachers reported that participation in the JCSP made a difference to the teaching methodologies they employ with non-JCSP classes.
- Students' participation in lessons was heavily influenced by the attention given to individual students by teachers and by the degree of involvement of each student in their own learning.
- Insufficient attention was given to monitoring attendance and punctuality. There was no evidence of attendance being monitored in thirty-one per cent of lessons observed.
- Profiling was used to assess students' progress in eighty per cent of the schools that participated in this evaluation.
- Standardised tests were used to track students' progress in literacy and numeracy in more than half of the schools that participated in the evaluation. Resource and learning-support teachers play a central role in most schools with regard to the assessment of these skills.

11.7.2 Recommendations for schools

- Schools should be cognisant of the textbooks and other resources that they use with JCSP students and ensure that they are appropriate to the students' needs, interests and ability levels. The subjects, themes and language of textbooks, for example, should be appropriate to students' age and ability levels.
- The profiling system should be planned, organised and co-ordinated to ensure that there is a consistent approach to it by relevant staff. Profiling should be used to inform planning for teaching and learning, and it should be implemented with all students in the JCSP.
- Greater attention needs to be given to the development of both literacy and numeracy skills in the classroom. This emphasis should permeate all areas of the JCSP. Also, the personal and social development of students should be prioritised in all lessons, with use being made of appropriate profiling statements.
- Evidence of students' progress, including the achievement of learning targets, should be accessible to students, teachers, and parents alike.
- Planning for students with special educational needs should involve subject and specialist teachers.

- Greater attention needs to be given to monitoring students' attendance and punctuality in lessons. Schools should devise a system of centrally administering attendance and punctuality data and communicating it to the home.
- All teaching and learning in the JCSP should have clarity of purpose, provide opportunities for students' participation and take account of student assessment outcomes.
- The outcomes of assessment should inform the selection of profiling statements and learning targets. Students should be made aware of their progress in all subject areas.
- Schools should devise ways of continuously recognising students' effort and achievement.

11.7.3 Recommendations for policy-makers and policy advisers

- Teaching methodologies need to be tailored more to the needs and interests of students. Teachers should be supported in this task by a whole-school emphasis on quality in teaching and learning. The JCSP Support Service can play an important role in this area.

11.8 Outcomes of the JCSP

11.8.1 Findings

- It was reported by various JCSP school personnel that the programme contributed to enhanced student attendance and retention at school. In the absence of relevant concrete data it is difficult to corroborate this finding. Notwithstanding this, in the majority of schools that participated in this evaluation there was evidence to suggest that the JCSP was having a positive impact on student retention levels. In the majority of cases this was because of the many strategies that schools had put in place to closely monitor attendance and punctuality. A small number of inspection reports, however, made reference to poor student attendance and punctuality.
- It was reported by JCSP school personnel that the programme contributed to enhanced literacy and numeracy skills among students. JCSP co-ordinators and teachers reported placing an emphasis on the development of literacy and numeracy skills in JCSP lessons. However, this did not hold true for the 108 lessons observed and rated for attention to literacy and numeracy.
- JCSP personnel reported that the programme contributed towards enhanced student motivation and attitude towards their schooling, and also towards developing their social skills. In the main, inspections corroborated these reports following their discussions and interactions with students.
- There are indicators, based predominantly on the views of schools' JCSP personnel, but also on data held by the Department of Education and Science and SEC, that the JCSP is successful at retaining students in school who might have otherwise left before the end of their junior cycle. This brings students face to face with the Junior Certificate examination and so can encourage them to sit the examination and achieve in it. The majority of students sat all or most of their subjects in their Junior Certificate examination.
- JCSP personnel reported that the programme contributed to enhanced home-school-community links; that it provided opportunities for students to enjoy and celebrate their learning; it encouraged the use of varied and alternative teaching strategies; and it encouraged teamwork among members of the teaching staff in schools.

11.8.2 Recommendations for schools

- In order to effectively evaluate the impact of the JCSP on student retention and attendance it is important that individual schools maintain detailed records regarding student enrolments and engage in their own analysis of these data.
- Schools should track the destination of JCSP students who do not progress to the senior cycle. This information could also be used to assess the success, or otherwise, of the programme.
- Schools should endeavour, in accordance with best practice, to regularly elicit the views of their students regarding the programme they offer them. This could be done by including students in the review of a school's programme.
- Given the significance to students of the nature of interactions between teachers and students, as well as the fact that all teachers are be able to contribute to the development of students' social and personal skills, all JCSP staff, but especially the JCSP teaching team, should be involved in choosing and awarding to students the social and personal development profiling statements.
- To measure the impact of the JCSP on students' literacy and numeracy, consideration should be given to regular use of standardised tests by schools participating in the programme.

11.8.3 Recommendations for policy-makers and policy advisers

- The development of students' social skills should continue to be a main emphasis of the JCSP.

Bibliography

Conference of Religious in Ireland, Education Commission, *Religious Congregations in Irish Education: A Role for the Future?* (Dublin: CORI, 1997).

Cosgrove, Judith, et. al., *Education for Life: The Achievements of 15-Year-Olds in Ireland in the Second Cycle of PISA* (Dublin: Educational Research Centre, 2005).

Department of Education and Science (Ireland), DEIS – *Delivering Equality Of Opportunity In Schools, An Action Plan for Educational Inclusion*, (Dublin: Government Publications, May 2005)

Junior Certificate School Programme Support Service, *About JCSP: Junior Certificate School Programme* (Dublin: Curriculum Development Unit, 2004).

National Council for Curriculum and Assessment, *Junior Cycle Review: Progress Report: Issues and Options for Development* (Dublin: Government Publications, 1999).

National Council for Curriculum and Assessment, *Research in Support of the Review of the Junior Certificate School Programme: Report by Nexus* (unpublished report, 2002).

National Economic and Social Forum, *Early School Leavers and Youth Unemployment*, Forum Report No. 11, (Dublin: Government publications, 1997).

National Economic and Social Forum, *Early School Leavers*, Forum Report No. 24, (Dublin: Government publications, 2002).

Appendix 1

Department of Education and Science
Circular M28/96
Circular M44/00

An Roinn Oideachais,
Brainse an Iarbhunoideachais,
Urlár,
Teach Háicín,
Baile Atha Cliath 2.
Tel: (01) 8734700
Fax:(01) 6777342

To: Boards of Management/Authorities of Second-Level Schools.

M28/96

Information Note on the Junior Certificate Elementary Programme

Introduction

The White Paper on Education, *Charting our Education Future*, indicated that it was intended to introduce an additional Junior Certificate Programme designed to reach out more effectively to a small but important minority of students whose particular needs are not adequately catered for in the present broadly based Junior Certificate.

Implementation

The Minister for Education has approved the introduction of the **Junior Certificate Elementary Programme** which is to be introduced in three phases. The first phase will commence in September 1996 with up to 45 schools delivering the programme. It is intended that the number of participating schools will increase to 80 over the next two phases. The 32 schools which have already participated in the Pilot Phase will be invited to introduce the Junior Certificate Elementary Programme in September 1996.

Underlying Principles

The Junior Certificate Elementary Programme offers an alternative pathway towards the aims and educational standards of the Junior Certificate for students at second level who:
- have serious difficulties with basic skills, including literacy and numeracy, which interfere with their ability to cope with normal demands of school and of everyday life;
- have repeatedly experienced failure during their school career and suffer form lack of confidence and low self –esteem;
- may be at risk of leaving school before the end of the junior cycle and thereby miss the opportunity of sitting Junior Certificate examinations.

Development

Development work on the programme was carried out by the Curriculum Development Unit of the City of Dublin Vocational Education Committee in consultation with the National Council for Curriculum and Assessment and the Department of Education and Science.

Support Service

A support service for schools which will provide information on the Programme and which will assist schools with the implementation of the Programme has been established. The support service is located in the Curriculum Development Unit of the City of Dublin VEC.

Enquiries regarding the programme should be directed to:

The Support Service
Junior Certificate Elementary Programme
Curriculum Development Unit
City of Dublin V.E.C.
Sundrive Road
Dublin 12

Telephone Number: (01) 453 5487
Fax Number: (01) 453 7659

Guidelines

Guidelines for schools have been prepared and a copy in enclosed for information.

A student profiling system, which is an integral part of the programme, is currently in preparation and will be available for the 1996/97 school year.

Resources

In addition to existing resources, the staffing allocation for schools approved to offer the Junior Certificate Elementary Programme will be on the basis of an additional 0.25 of a teaching resource per school.

A special per capita grant of £50 will be made, once only, in respect of each student entering the programme in schools in the free education scheme.

Copies of circular

School authorities are requested to provide a copy of this letter to the parents' and teachers' representatives on the Board of Management, where such exists, or to the parents' association/National Parents' Council representatives or other appropriate representatives of the parents/teachers for transmission to individual parents and teachers.

An Roinn Oideachais agus Eolaíochta,
Brainse an Iarbhunoideachais
Urlár 3,
Teach Háicín,
Baile Atha Cliath 2.

Tel: (01) 8892041
Fax:(01) 809 5048

To: Management Authorities of Second-Level Schools.

M44/00

Expansion of the Junior Certificate School Programme and
Improved Teacher Resources to Apply from 2000/01

1. The Junior Certificate School Programme was introduced in September 1996. The programme has been developed on a phased basis since then. There are 85 schools/centres offering the programme at present. The Programme is being extended to a number of schools operating the "Stay in School Retention Initiative". These schools have already been invited to deliver the programme.

2. Schools approved for participation in JCSP for the first time in the school year 2000/01 or subsequent school years, will be restricted to a maximum of 45 approved places in each of the first three school years.

3. Individual schools participating in JCSP will, with effect from the commencement of the 2000/01 school year, receive an improved allocation. This allocation will be at the rate of 0.25 whole-time teacher equivalent (WTE) per group of 45 students participating in JCSP and will be applied in the following manner:

Students	WTE
45 or fewer	0.25
46 to 90	0.50
91 to 135	0.75

(Previously participating schools received an additional 0.25 WTE per school regardless of student numbers.)

4. This allocation will normally be made on the basis of the numbers of recognised students enrolled in JCSP on 30th September of the previous school year and who are entered on the October Lists. Allocations may be adjusted, where necessary, to take account of significant fluctuation (increase/decrease) in projected numbers of participating students for the following school year. In any event, the number of students on which this allocation may be based will be limited to the number of JCSP places approved by the Department.

5. Please provide a copy of this circular to the appropriate representatives of parents and teachers for transmission to individual parents and teachers.

Appendix 2

Follow-up to the JCSP evaluation (April 2004)

The thirty schools that participated in the evaluation of the JCSP were informed verbally at the time of the evaluation, and subsequently by letter, that there would be a follow-up to the evaluation. This follow-up evaluation took place in April 2004; twenty-nine of the thirty schools or centres for education were involved in the follow-up evaluation.

In preparation for the follow-up, schools were requested by letter in January 2004 to submit a report to the Department of Education and Science on progress made in implementing the recommendations made in the schools' original JCSP evaluation report. They were asked to rate themselves, on a scale of one to four, on progress made in implementing each of the recommendations in this report, and to comment on the progress made in implementing recommendations. The four-point scale is as follows:

1: Little or no progress has been made
2: Some progress has been made; however, weaknesses outweigh strengths
3: Significant progress has been made in implementing recommendation, but progress has not been made on all key issues
4: Recommendation is fully implemented

As part of the follow-up evaluation, inspectors reviewed the schools' own accounts of the progress they had made in implementing the recommendations. After the follow-up evaluation visit the inspectors then reviewed the schools' applied rating and either corroborated it or adjusted the rating as necessary. A short report on the follow-up evaluation was then sent to each school.

The following table gives a list of the recommendations most frequently made in all thirty schools evaluated.

Recommendations	Frequency
To make provision for continuous review of the programme	20
To adopt written policies for literacy and numeracy	15
To integrate literacy and numeracy throughout the curriculum	15
Better profiling	15
To engage in more appropriate teaching methods	12
To pursue in-career development courses relevant to the JCSP	9
Greater involvement of specialist staff (core team)	9
Parents and feeder primary schools to be consulted with regard to selection of students	9
More comprehensive records	8
To address the cross-curricular aims of the programme	8
To include information technology on the curriculum	8
To involve more teachers in the planning of the programme	6
Review of student selection procedures	7
To use JCSP postcards more frequently	6
Involvement of guidance counsellors	6

Implementation of recommendations

An analysis of the inspectors' reports revealed that ninety-four (or forty per cent) of the 237 recommendations were found to have been implemented fully. These received a rating of four. The specific nature of these recommendations is described below.

Recommendation	Number of 4 ratings	Frequency of recommendation
Provision for continuous review of the JCSP	7	20
More involvement with ICD	7	9
More detailed records of JCSP	7	8
Better profiling	6	15
Greater involvement of specialist staff (core team)	5	9
Better use of time	4	4
All subject teachers to be involved in planning the programme	4	6
Use ICT as a teaching tool	4	8
Parents and feeder primary schools to be consulted with regard to selection of students	4	9
Appropriate teaching and learning strategies	4	12
Review of student selection procedures	4	7
JCSP to be included on agenda of staff meetings	3	3
Clear job specification for JCSP co-ordinator	3	4
Appoint JCSP core team	3	3
Specific JCSP events to be introduced	3	4
Diagnostic tests to be administered regularly	3	3
Allocation of dedicated co-ordinator time	2	2
Develop formal plan for the JCSP	2	5
Formal team meetings	2	3
Examine JCSP to provide a more limited curriculum	2	5
Strategies to be adopted for maintaining and developing positive aspects of programme	2	2
Consider providing LCA	2	2
Timetabling of library sessions	2	2
More use of JCSP postcards	2	6
Monitoring of attendance and punctuality	2	4
Review of mandatory transition year programme	1	1
Development of numeracy skills to be given priority throughout the JCSP	1	15
Consider designated JCSP class	1	1
More collaborative approach and creative cross-curricular links recommended	1	8
Material within Irish cultural studies to be chosen to reflect the interests of students	1	1

An analysis of the inspectors' reports revealed that there were twenty-one (eleven per cent) out of a total of 237 recommendations where little or no progress was made in implementing recommendations. These received a rating of one from the inspectors. The table below shows the type of recommendations that received a rating of one from the inspectors.

Recommendation	Frequency of recommendation
Full review of programme	3
Exploring ways to provide more time for planning and profiling	1
Timetable co-ordinator for at least one class period with each JCSP group	1
Timetable core subjects in the morning	1
Reduce number of teachers for each JCSP class	1
Draw up agenda for team meetings, and record decisions	1
Avail of ICD	1
Focused in-service training on theme of multiple intelligences to be provided	1
More use of ICT in classes	1
Written literacy and numeracy policy to be drawn up	2
Need to draft literacy policy	2
Individual education plans need to be designed for some students	1
List of guest speakers to be drawn up	1
Bring outside speakers into school for JCSP	1
Should be contact between career guidance personnel and third-year JCSP	1
Consideration given to introducing paired reading for first-year JCSP classes	1
Draw up detailed plan for JCSP	1

In summary, approximately half (115) of the 237 recommendations received a rating of either four or one. This means that work was still in progress on implementing half (122) of the recommendations made in the evaluation reports.

Appendix 3

Details of ICD Courses Provided by JCSP Support Service 1996–2003

September to December 1996
Implementation of the JCEP and the profiling Programme
Review of English
Review of Maths
Profiling and feedback to parents and pupils
Action for life: PE teachers
Co-ordinator meetings x 2
Team Building and cross curricular work
Literacy awareness across the curriculum

September to December 1997
Implementation of the Programme and the profiling system
Co-ordinators Meeting x 2
Parental involvement
Methodologies and new approaches to teaching the Junior Certificate
Literacy awareness across the curriculum x 3
Teaching Junior Certificate Mathematics to Reluctant Learners x 2
Teaching Gaeilge to reluctant learners x 2
Physical Education
Subject reviews in 15 subjects
Teaching Styles and Methodologies

January to June 1998
Maths
Gaeilge
Co-ordinators Meeting x 3
Review Meetings:
History, Geography
Religion, Keyboard
Metalwork, Woodwork,
Home Economics, Art
Maths Meeting
Follow-up to Review Meeting:
History, Geography,
Religion, Information Technology,
Metalwork, Woodwork,
Home Economics, Art
Computer In-Service
Maths Meeting
Subject Review Meeting
Technical Graphics
Co-ordinators Meeting x 3
Parental Involvement
Irish Cultural Studies Meeting

September to December 1998
Implementation of the Programme and the profiling system
Computers and the JCSP
Review of Science, Business Studies, Music, Technology and foreign language
The Cross Curricular/thematic approach and teambuilding
Communications and Confidence Building
Co-ordinators Meeting and in-service on facilitation Skills
Co-ordinators Meeting and in-service on facilitation Skills
Outdoor Education
Drama: a medium for learning
Literacy across the curriculum.
Teaching Irish to reluctant students.
Teaching Materials Technology (Wood) and Metalwork to reluctant students.
Teaching Home Economics to reluctant students.
Introduction to using computer software in the JCSP
Introduction to using the internet with JCSP students

January to June 1999
Teaching Materials Technology (Wood) and Metalwork
Co-ordinators' Meeting
Drama for Personal Development: Workshop 3
Make a Book: Launch and Information Meeting
Facilitation Skills: Development of Skills, the Next Stage.
Science, Technology and Business Studies Review
Parental Involvement and Transfer Programmes
Co-ordinators' Meeting
Learning Curve Communication and Confidence Building: 'Making Friends with School'
'Make A Book' Exhibition

September to December 1999
Implementation Meeting for Schools new to the Programme
Development of Art Statement linking with Museums
Limerick Meeting
Cork Meeting
Computer Software and the Internet
Co-ordinators' Meeting x 3
Review of Science Statements (2nd Meeting)
Waterford Meeting
Literacy Across the Curriculum
Teaching Junior Certificate Mathematics to Reluctant Learners
Galway Meeting
The Students, the Artist and the Museum

January to June 2000
Introduction to Make a Book Project
Co-ordinators' Meeting x 3
Increase your Mind Power: Thinking Skills for Students
"Honey, I blew up the 2nd years": Science for JCSP students
Review of Business Studies Statements
Launch of Make a Book Exhibition
Make a Book Exhibition
Co-ordinators' Meeting Dublin x 3
Principals' Consultative Meeting x 3
Information Meeting for Schools New to the Programme

September to December 2000
Introduction and Implementation Meeting for New Schools
Co-ordinators' Meeting x 3
The Cross Curricular approach and Teamwork
Self Esteem and Effective Learning in every Classroom
Learning Curve: Communication and Confidence Building
Introduction to Facilitation Skills
Teaching Irish to JCSP students: Bonn Leibheil and Cultural Studies
Literacy across the Curriculum

January to June 2001
Development of SPHE Statements
Introduction to Make a Book Project
Co-ordinators' Meeting x 3
Literacy Across the Curriculum
The JCSP and Traveller Education
Home Economics
Introduction and Implementation of the Junior Certificate School Programme
The Junior Certificate School Programme and Mixed Ability Issues
Launch of Make a Book Exhibition
Co-ordinators' Meeting x 3
Drama in Education Teach your subject through this active learning strategy.

September to December 2001
Implementation meeting for new co-ordinators
Teaching Home Economics to JCSP Students
Donegal Cluster Meeting
Review of the Religious Education Statements
The JCSP and Traveller Education
Co-ordinators Meeting x3
The JCSP and Cross Curricular issues
Bridging the gap: The class tutor and the JCSP Student
Galway Cluster Meeting
Monaghan Cluster Meeting
Teaching History to JCSP Students
Kerry Cluster Meeting

January to June 2002
Make A Book Introduction to schools participating in the student event
Local Progress Meetings
Co-ordinators' Meeting x 3
Managing challenging behaviour through choice theory
Local Progress Meetings
A School Wide Approach to Literacy
Solution Focus Thinking
Local Progress Meetings
Numeracy, Maths Review and the JCSP
Launch and Exhibition Make A Book
Co-ordinators' Meeting for those new to profiling x 3
Introduction to the Implementation of the JCSP for schools intending to join the Programme

September to December 2002
Introductory Meeting for Schools New to the JCSP
Emergent Literacy and the potential early leaver: A whole school Approach to literacy
Numeracy, Maths Review and the JCSP
Cross Curricular and Thematic Teaching
Co-ordinators' Meeting x 3
Teaching French to JCSP students
Inter-culturalism
Solution focused Thinking
Creating a Positive Learning Environment
Emergent Literacy and the potential early leaver: A whole school Approach to literacy
Teaching Gaeilge to reluctant learners

January to June 2003
Make A Book Introduction to participating in the event
Cross Curricular Approach
Local Progress Meetings
Co-ordinators' Meeting x 3
A School Wide Approach to Literacy
Cross Curricular Approach
Using ICT with JCSP Students
The Arts and The Junior Cycle
Teaching Gaeilge to JCSP students
Review of English Statements
Exploring Mixed Ability within the JCSP
Special Education and JCSP
Geography Review
Literacy Research Projects: Whole School Approach
Parents and learning in Junior Cycle
Drama in the classroom
Launch and Exhibition Make A Book
Co-ordinators' Meeting x 3
Introduction to the Implementation of the Junior Certificate School Programme for schools intending to join the Programme

September–December 2003
Implementation Meeting for Schools New to the JCSP and New Co-ordinators
JCSP Initiatives Briefing
Co-ordinators' Meeting x 3
Cross Curricular and Thematic Teaching
Materials Technology: Wood and Metal and Technical Graphics
Literacy and the potential early leaver: A school wide approach to literacy
Making Numeracy and Mathematics Meaningful for Reluctant Learners
Mixed Ability Workshop
Solution Focused Brief Therapy: An effective strategy for dealing with difficult behaviour.
Business Studies and JCSP students
Teaching Gaeilge to Reluctant learners

Appendix 4

Time allocated to different subjects in the JCSP curriculum in the schools evaluated

Subject	First Year	Second Year	Third Year
English	100	100	100
Mathematics	100	100	100
Irish	38.5	40	52
Irish cultural studies	57.7	56	40
Modern language	26.9	20	16
Science	38.5	48	40
Technology/ technical graphics	19.2	20	20
Metalwork	30.8	48	52
MT wood	46.2	56	64
Art and craft	88.5	88	88
Drama, dance, choir	7.7	12	0
Music	15.4	32	24
Social education	30.8	28	16
CSPE	65.4	68	68
SPHE	50	48	40
PE	88.5	84	88
Home economics	80.8	76	76
Business studies	15.4	12	24
Computer studies	61.5	60	52
Geography	53.8	48	40
History	42.3	36	36
Religion	92.3	92	92
Reading	7.7	8	8

Table 8A Proportion of schools responding that have subject in JCSP curriculum in first, second and third year

Subject	Time (minutes)				
	1–120	121–180	181–240	241–300	300+
English	3.8	23.1	46.2	15.4	11.5
Mathematics	3.8	26.9	50.0	15.4	3.8
Irish	15.3	15.4	7.7	0	0
Irish cultural studies	34.5	19.2	3.8		
Modern language	11.5	15.4			
Science	11.4	26.9			
Technology/ technical graphics	3.8	11.5		3.8	
Metalwork	11.5	15.4	3.8		
MT wood	15.3	26.9	3.8		
Art and craft	38.5	46.2	3.8		
Drama, dance, choir	3.8	3.8			
Music	11.5	3.8			
Social education	19.2	7.7	3.8		
CSPE	65.3				
SPHE	50				
PE	84.6	3.8			
Home economics	34.6	38.5	7.7		
Business studies	7.6	7.7			
Computer studies	49.9	3.8	7.7		
Geography	46.1	7.7			
History	34.6	7.7			
Religion	88.5	3.8			
Reading	3.8	3.8			

Table 8B Time per week allocated to subjects in first-year JCSP: proportion of classes for which data is available

Subject	Time (minutes)				
	1–120	121–180	181–240	241–300	300+
English	4.0	24.0	56.0	12.0	4.0
Mathematics	4.0	28.0	52.0	12.0	4.0
Irish	20	12	8		
Irish cultural studies	28	20	8		
Modern language	12	8			
Science	24	24			
Technology/technical graphics		16		4	
Metalwork	16	32			
MT wood	8	40	8		
Art and craft	36	44	8		
Drama, dance, choir	12				
Music	34	8			
Social education	12	12	4		
CSPE	68				
SPHE	48				
PE	76	8			
Home economics	28	44	4		
Business studies	8	4			
Computer studies	48	8	4		
Geography	32	16			
History	36				
Religion	88	4			
Reading	8				

Table 8C Time per week allocated to subjects in second-year JCSP: proportion of classes for which data is available

Subject	Time (minutes)				
	1–120	121–180	181–240	241–300	300+
English	4.0	20.0	44.0	16.0	16.0
Mathematics	4.0	28.0	56.0	8.0	4.0
Irish	20	24	8		
Irish cultural studies	36	4			
Modern language	12	4			
Science	24	12	4		
Technology/technical graphics	12	8			
Metalwork	12	28	12		
MT wood	12	44	8		
Art and craft	16	68	4		
Drama, dance, choir	0	0	0	0	0
Music	16	8			
Social education	4	8	4		
CSPE	68				
SPHE	40				
PE	80	8			
Home economics	24	40	12		
Business studies	8	16			
Computer studies	48	4			
Geography	32	4	4		
History	24	12			
Religion	84	8			
Reading	4	4			

Table 8D Time per week allocated to subjects in third-year JCSP: proportion of classes for which data is available